Praise for *Submerged*

"*Submerged* is a tidal wave that will leave you feeling as if you are drowning only to provide a lifeline to stable ground. Sheena King painstakingly notes how sexual predators and family violence deepen the wells of despair and expand violence and childhood trauma. Her memoir notes the casualties of damaged children, women, and men and family members. King and the poets who contribute to this important text offer a raw record of memory, shame, and rage. They ask for and offer accountability. Their caretaking as healers acknowledges vulnerabilities and violations of incarcerated women; this author and her community aids and educates everyone with this powerful book of rage and sorrow, death, and redemption. Anchored in revolutionary and transformative love, *Submerged* also allows us to swim to shore with our souls intact."

—Joy James, author of *In Pursuit of Revolutionary Love* and *New Bones Abolition: Captive Maternal Agency and the (After)life of Erica Garner*

"Powerful. A moving and heartbreaking tale of innocence lost, two lives destroyed, and one woman's incredible journey to redemption behind prison walls."

—Tammy Mal, author of *Convenient Suspect* and *Little Girl Lost*

"*Submerged* proves that while you can sink to the depths, you can also rise back up through the power of testimony. Searing, it hurts, yet it is so worth it to read. Sheena King's book is going to help a lot of people."

—Jennifer Black, coeditor of *Beneath the Mountain: An Anti-Prison Reader*

"Throughout this spirited, harrowing, and unflinching memoir, Sheena King honors us with her personal saga, in vivid prose and poetry, describing a gifted woman who endured hellish childhood sexual trauma and deprivation, resulting in actions that derailed her life and landed her in prison—yet which also led her, through group therapies and brave introspection, to a path of transformational knowledge, faith, resilience, love, and self-redemption. A testament to recovery from terrible abuses, she offers this book in a heartfelt desire to assist others in similar need of healing. Written with impressive narrative skill, *Submerged* will challenge you, haunt you, and—by the very fact that Sheena King managed against formidable odds to create this powerful memoir—bolster your faith that a person not only can survive the unsurvivable, but triumph."

—Reverend Steve Kanji Ruhl, MDiv, author of the award-winning memoir *Appalachian Zen*

"Sheena King's *Submerged* is unflinchingly honest, hard to read, and impossible to look away from. King's story brings the abuse-to-prison pipeline to life, describing how the horror of child sexual abuse ultimately led to the very different horror of incarceration. Just as importantly, though, *Submerged* highlights how much King and the women she is incarcerated with have learned, grown, and could offer to society now, if only we are willing to see them for who they are rather than what they were convicted of."

—Leigh Goodmark, author of *Imperfect Victims: Criminalized Survivors and the Promise of Abolition Feminism*

"Sheena's way of creatively sharing her story with us is inspiring. The truth, challenge, and triumph, all entwined, keeps the reader engrossed in the storyline and makes us seek more. She was meant to be a writer. Cheers to what's next!"

—Terri Harper, inmate serving a life sentence at SCI Muncy in Muncy, Pennsylvania, and editor of *The Movement* magazine

"It is hard to believe that one life story can encapsule both deep pain and profound love—sometimes simultaneously. In fact, some may think that it is impossible that strength and redemption can grow and maybe even flourish from degradation and abuse. Indeed, it may be the case that only survivors of horrific violence and people living under the vicious control of the carceral state (and their advocates) can really understand what gender violence and mass criminalization means. But if there is any possibility, then Ms. King's memoir *Submerged* offers us the best hope for building a movement of understanding and resistance. Not uncomplicated or uncontroversial, the book is as painful as it is inspiring and as troubling as it is hopeful. But the message is clear: survivors' stories told through personal accounts and poems will not only teach us but lead us to work for justice and freedom like we have never worked before. For that, I am both moved and grateful."

—Beth Richie, author of *Arrested Justice: Black Women, Violence, and America's Prison Nation* and coauthor of *Abolition. Feminism. Now.* with Angela Davis and others

"By narrating her endurance and survival of childhood sexual abuse in *Submerged*, Sheena King beams twin lights: the harsh light of truth, and the warming light that comes when trauma is no longer hidden in darkness but seen, shared, and in the process of being healed. *Submerged* is a memoir of resilience, love, and the enduring will to fight one's way to the surface and breathe."

—K.A. Hays, author of *Windthrow* and other books and associate professor of Creative Writing, Bucknell University

"Most of us are careful to avoid painful memories, but Sheena King faces the piercing traumas of her life with clear-eyed and heartbreaking honesty. In *Submerged* she writes poignantly and powerfully about the soul-crushing experiences of her youth—but also about her imprisonment, her growth and change, and her discovery of deep and lasting spirituality and love. Hers is a hard-earned peace, and we, as readers, are the beneficiaries of her journey to healing and hope. She has given us an unforgettable account of despair and discovery, forgiveness and hope."

—Joyce Hinnefeld, emerita professor of English at Moravian University, program facilitator at Shining Light, and author of *The Dime Museum* and other works of fiction and nonfiction

"With fearless honesty, Sheena King plunges us into the darkness of her childhood sexual abuse and shows us how soul-crushing and hidden trauma morphs a life of promise into a life sentence at the Muncy State Prison housing women in central Pennsylvania. With humility and abiding faith, she recounts her experiences of deep personal evolution, healing, and love in a place antithetical to these pursuits, and her commitment to channel her strength and wisdom into helping others heal. *Submerged* weaves poetry and prose into a provocative narrative, witnessing how courage and emotional fortitude can dispel the darkest shadows and restore the light."

—Jennifer Hwozdek, teaching artist at Life Out Loud, a trauma-informed storytelling program serving incarcerated women, and codirector of Ridgelines Language Arts

Submerged

On Healing from Abuse While Navigating a Lifetime of Imprisonment

Sheena King

Submerged: On Healing from Abuse While Navigating a Lifetime of Imprisonment

ISBN: 979–8–88744–134–4 (paperback)
ISBN: 979–8–88744–135–1 (ebook)
Library of Congress Control Number: 2025931386

Cover design by John Yates / stealworks.com
Interior design by briandesign
Author illustration by Anna Sorokina

10 9 8 7 6 5 4 3 2 1

PM Press
PO Box 23912
Oakland, CA 94623
www.pmpress.org

Printed in the USA.

You open your mouth to scream—
shut it, since there is no one listening.

Submerged is a work of nonfiction.

This book is dedicated to God for the strength and the gift and to the people He has placed on this path with me.

Contents

Poems

Foreword

Rikeyah Lindsay

Submerged is an invitation! It calls us in at a time dense with indifference and invites us to cast aside nonchalance and open our hearts to get to know Sheena King, the person. Then it compels us to open our minds and journey with Sheena as she, along with other women who bravely share their own stories, offers us vulnerable accounts of harms endured (and caused) on their way to healing. Sheena actively challenges deeply ingrained ideas about all of this and, ultimately, about justice itself, providing a landscape in which we can examine and interrogate the root causes of violence. Within the world Sheena shares with us, we can reflect on what true prevention and intervention look like. She opens a door through which we can move beyond the cultural inclination to rush to judgment and cookie-cutter prescriptions of punishment. She creates space for new ideas and new ways of healing.

While Sheena has penned a powerful, moving narrative, we must remember that her story is part of a collective experience shared by far too many women, especially Black women—and in the Black community not only by women. This book pulls together the threads of survival in the face of systemic racism, white supremacy, and violence. We are all survivors of a system with a nonstop quest to eliminate and exterminate Black people. This truth rings throughout Black communities in the US. From the moment the very first Africans were taken into captivity and transported to the Americas, Africans have endured some of the most vile and inhumane treatment imaginable. Families were ripped away from each other; men were beaten savagely; women were raped mercilessly. These historical traumas live deep in the bloodlines of the descendants of the enslaved and are continuously compounded by the everyday struggle for survival in Black and other intentionally underresourced communities across the country. Historical and present-day traumas show up in our communities as monsters we are often too afraid to speak about. They show up as alcoholism, drug abuse, sexual violence, sexual promiscuity, cutting, child abuse, neglect, and more. Sheena King shines a spotlight on these monsters by providing an unflinching examination essential for healing—both hers and ours.

The monsters scar and permanently change us on a molecular level, often before our brains have the chance to reach maturity and full development. *Submerged* paints a stark picture as Sheena shares the effects of exposure to violence and harm at the most formative points in life. Science tells us that trauma impacts a person's ability to make sound decisions. Science also tells us that brains don't reach full development until between the ages of twenty-five and twenty-seven. We know, through studies like Adverse Childhood Experiences (ACEs), that a child's early exposure to negligence and violence can predetermine their own propensity toward violence, which in turn predicts the probability of contact with the (criminal) legal system.

Sheena's memoir is a heart-wrenching chronicle of the effects of early childhood trauma. It's a crystal clear account of how trauma, especially trauma experienced early on in life, can alter our ways of thinking, numb our senses to pain, and detach us from the ramifications of our actions. It's a firsthand account of how unprotected we are, even in our own homes, and how that lack of protection creates lasting effects on our lives and the lives of others. It's an acknowledgment of harm endured and inflicted. It's a reflection of healing in spite of yourself and your circumstances. It reveals the truth about the criminal legal system's inability to heal or rehabilitate while uplifting the impact that can be made when we acknowledge, explore, and unpack our traumas and resolve to walk in healing.

And what does this country offer as a solution when people succumb to their traumas? *Prison!* The powers that be, who have never been accountable to anything, would have us believe that the criminal legal system is the answer to stopping violence. We have run the saying that "violence creates more violence" into the ground. Yet, with all the facts and details of the history of violence endured by Blacks at the hands of this system, there has never been a conversation or an attempt to shift the focus to the healing of the Black community itself. Instead, Black people are brutalized and penalized excessively when we succumb to our trauma. No one considers the circumstances that lead to violence, especially when the person responsible for causing the harm is Black. The empathetic thought process that "hurt people hurt people" is easily replaced with thoughts of "you did the crime, you do the time." But doing the time will never promote or sustain healing. On the contrary, prisons in and of themselves only do the work of exacerbating violence in communities by removing members and exposing them to even more violent and harmful circumstances.

Even with decades of data and evidence that support the need to abolish prisons, this country continues to incarcerate those who have been most harmed by its own system of negligence, violence, and destruction. We cannot afford to accept these lies as inevitabilities, as the way things have to be.

As you read these pages, Sheena will encourage you to ask questions:

- What was the original harm?
- Who was responsible?
- Where were the points of intervention that went unaddressed?
- What role does the criminal legal system play?

In *Submerged*, we are forced to know that Sheena King was not safe even though prisons supposedly exist to keep us safe, just as we know that our communities are not safer because of the existence of prisons. As you read the accounts of trauma, harm, accountability, and change in these pages, challenge yourself to imagine what a system of true safety, healing, and justice will look like. Imagine what we can—what we must—create to replace a failed system that deepens the circles and cycles of violence with each generation.

Sheena is a survivor. We are all survivors of a failed system. Yet, like Sheena, we must take our collective healing seriously, interrogating the root causes and demanding accountability not only for ourselves but also for the systems that create the conditions in which so much harm can occur.

Introduction

Victoria Law

Sheena King was born in 1972. Hip-hop had not yet been born. Neither had many of the laws that would turn the United States into the world's prison nation.[1] That year, the US incarcerated 6,269 women in its state and federal prisons.[2]

Sheena starts her childhood recollections in 1981. That year, she turned nine years old. Incarceration was already swelling—the same year, the nation's entire prison population grew by almost 40,000 people (mostly men), bringing the nation's prison population to a record high of 369,000. Fewer than 15,000 state and federal prisoners were women, but their ranks would also skyrocket in the coming years.

The number of people sentenced to life (and death) behind bars across the US has nearly quintupled since then.

Now, more than 200,000 people—or one of every 7 people in prison—are serving life sentences in the United States. One of every 15 women is serving a life sentence—and, in recent years, the number of women sentenced to life without parole has increased at nearly double that of men. Like all things prison, these sentences have disproportionately been meted out to Black women—one in

---

1 Beth Richie coined the term *prison nation* to refer to not only the skyrocketing numbers of people behind bars but also the ideological and public policy shifts that respond to social problems with criminalization and punishment. For more, see Beth Richie, *Arrested Justice: Black Women, Violence, and America's Prison Nation* (New York University Press, 2012), 3.

2 Wendy Sawyer, "Table 1: Women's Prison and Jail Population Estimates and Incarceration Rates, 1922–2015," in "The Gender Divide: Tracking Women's State Prison Growth," Prison Policy Initiative, January 9, 2018, https://www.prisonpolicy.org/reports/women_overtime_table_1.html.

every 39 Black women (compared to one in 59 white women) in prison is serving a life-without-parole sentence.[3]

This includes Sheena, who was sentenced to life without parole in 1992. She was twenty years old.

Two years later, federal lawmakers passed the Violent Crime Control and Law Enforcement Act. The act encouraged states to pass more punitive sentencing laws and awarded federal funding for new prisons and jails in exchange for dramatically limiting "earned time" credits for incarcerated people. This last provision meant that no matter what strides a person had made behind bars, there was virtually no time awarded off their sentence for good behavior (or self-transformation).[4] That didn't apply to Sheena, whose only hope of relief would come either from the courts or the governor's mercy through clemency, but it did mean that the prison around her started to fill with more women serving longer sentences. Sheena herself notes this—when she entered prison in 1993, SCI Muncy incarcerated just over 600 women. By 2014, it confined over 1,500 women.

Women's incarceration has risen 525 percent between 1980 and 2021—a rate that is twice as high as that of men. The vast majority of incarcerated women have experienced trauma and violence, often repeatedly and often by people they loved and trusted. It's a pathway so common that it has a name: the abuse-to-prison pipeline.

That term didn't exist when Sheena was growing up, during the two years between her arrest and trial, or during the many years and court filings spent challenging her sentence. But, as she notes in this memoir, the majority of the hundreds of thousands of women churning through the prison system "have low

---

3 Trevariana Mason, "Extreme Sentences Disproportionately Impact and Harm Black Women," National Black Women's Justice Institute, September 23, 2021, https://www.nbwji.org/post/extreme-sentences-disproportionately-impact-and-harm-black-women.

4 Monique O. Ositelu, "Mass Incarceration in the U.S.," in "Equipping Individuals for Life Beyond Bars: The Promise of Higher Education and Job Training in Closing the Gap in Skills for Incarcerated Adults," New America, last updated November 4, 2019, https://www.newamerica.org/education-policy/reports/equipping-individuals-life-beyond-bars/mass-incarceration-in-the-us.

self-esteem, false bravado, codependency, and a deep yearning for love and acceptance."

Sheena's early life is a stark example. Even before she turned nine, her mother's boyfriend had started sexually abusing her. For years, she silently endured his assaults, believing his threats that not only would no one believe her, but that he would kill her sisters if she told. Her mother, who worked several jobs to keep their family afloat, had a temper that often led to physical beatings—and Sheena was afraid that telling her would result in more violence against her.

That trauma turned into a cycle that continued long after that particular man was chased out of her life. As Sheena grew into a teenager, she unwittingly replicated these same abusive dynamics with other boys and men. At age eighteen, she took another woman's life. Two years later, she was sentenced to life without parole.

This past year, she turned fifty-two years old.

I first connected with Sheena in 2018. She was on the hunt for newsletters, magazines, or any outlet that would consider publishing writings by incarcerated women. At the time, I was the editor and publisher of a zine called *Tenacious: Art and Writings by Women in Prison*. I don't recall much about our first few letters, but our exchange resulted in her short piece about mothering from prison in that year's Mother's Day issue.

A few months later, I was the one reaching out to her. I was working on an article about people sentenced to life without parole for crimes they had committed between the ages of eighteen and twenty-five and learned that she was one of them.

In 2012, the US Supreme Court had ruled that automatically sentencing juveniles, defined as those under age eighteen, to life without parole violated the Constitution's Eighth Amendment prohibition against cruel and unusual punishment. Four years later, in 2016, the court made its decision retroactive, enabling the nation's 2,300 juvenile lifers to file for resentencing.

In Pennsylvania, 2,723 lifers had been between the ages of eighteen and twenty-five when they committed their crimes.

They made up over half of the state's lifer population. Many were already in their fifties, sixties, and seventies and had spent their young adulthood, middle age, and now older age behind bars. Nonetheless, all were excluded from reconsideration simply based on their birthdays.

Sheena willingly shared her story for my article. She directed me to court documents corroborating the details that made it into the legal records. She answered all of my questions—and, as a journalist, I had many of them. She did not flinch from looking back at her thoughts, feelings, and fears at the time.

Within these pages, Sheena has chosen a different way of sharing her life. She does not elaborate on the events that led to her arrest and sentence. She does not attempt to relitigate the outcome of her court case or dispute the tragedy that she caused. When I asked why she omitted those details, she explained that, first and foremost, she did not want to retraumatize the family of her victim by recounting the details of their loss.

Instead, she wanted to write a book that exposed the repeated traumas that often silence women—and shape the paths they choose later in life. She hoped that, by pulling away the ill-healed scabs from her childhood, not only could she begin to heal, she could also help prevent others from reenacting the same destructive cycles. This is also why she includes poems by other incarcerated survivors throughout her pages, reminders in verse that her childhood and adolescent experiences are, tragically, shared by many others who end up ensnared within the carceral system.

For years, many of those women suffered in silence. Sometimes, a prison might offer a program to help work through their traumas. In some prisons, survivors themselves formed programs—and communities—to heal themselves and help heal others. Some of those groups even went on to advocate for mass release and changes in the law.[5] But all too often, survivors are left on their own to hide from these painful memories in an

5 Victoria Law, *Resistance Behind Bars: The Struggles of Incarcerated Women*, 2nd ed. (PM Press, 2012).

environment that often replicates the control and punishment dynamics of their abusive loved ones.

Now, thanks to Survived and Punished, a national network that provides resources for and organizes with abuse survivors entangled in the criminal legal system, there's also a name for those who have been pushed down that pathway: criminalized survivors.

Beth Richie, a cofounder of INCITE! Women, Gender Non-Conforming, and Trans People of Color Against Violence[6] and the author of multiple books examining the intersections of interpersonal and state violence against Black women, noted that the term focuses attention on the person's "relationship to the harm, not to the legal case. It says that one of the forms of abuse is the state criminalizing people's attempts to survive."[7]

The state not only criminalizes attempts to survive, it also erases many of the experiences that influenced survivors' lives. In her family memoir of the Chinese Exclusion Act, *Mott Street*, Ava Chin writes, "It is a general rule of thumb, among researchers and historians alike, that it is the written record that is the gold standard."[8]

But the written records on Sheena—and the hundreds of thousands of women behind bars—paint not only an incomplete but a distorted story. Combing through court filings, news reports, and prison records tells us about the worst decisions they have ever made and their tragic outcomes. These documents might show a photo or tell us their height, age, or complexion. Some records might include descriptions of tattoos and scars, or listings of previous convictions and sentences. But these records tell us nothing about their childhoods—whether those were happy times or years filled with traumas and fears. They tell us nothing about their hopes and dreams and how their experiences might have reshaped—or ground down—those early ambitions.

---

6 See more about INCITE! at https://incite-national.org.

7 Victoria Law, "'The Worst Abuser You Could Ever Have,'" *The Nation*, July 18, 2022, https://www.thenation.com/article/society/tracy-mccarter-suvived-punished.

8 Ava Chin, *Mott Street: A Chinese American Family's Story of Exclusion and Homecoming* (Penguin Press, 2023).

Also missing from those official documents are the many stories of resilience, perseverance, healing, and community, even in the bleakest of circumstances. Sheena writes about these experiences candidly and boldly. She unflinchingly travels down the roads of these painful early experiences, but to read her words is not just to be a voyeur. She takes her pain and transforms it into purpose—because in order for us to dismantle the abuse-to-prison pipeline, we must first acknowledge and understand how it works.

Thus, it is my honor to introduce these pages. Sheena's stories are often painful and unflinching, yet at the same time, they offer all of us hope and healing. As another criminalized survivor, serving a life sentence in Oklahoma, recently reminded me, "It's healing to help heal others."[9] And that's what Sheena's words are meant to do.

---

9 Victoria Law, "Oklahoma Gives Incarcerated Survivors of Domestic Violence a New Chance at Freedom," *Bolts*, May 24, 2024, https://boltsmag.org/oklahoma-survivors-act.

Preface

The number of children who have been sexually abused is staggering. The long-term effects of child molestation and abuse on children is devastatingly depressing. We cannot pretend that it doesn't happen or close our eyes to the truth. You may have suffered at the hands of an adult in the past, or you may be living through that nightmare right now. You're not alone. Perhaps you love someone who is now trying to cope with the debilitating effects of trauma. You don't know how to help. Your mind can't conceive of what she or he has been through.

You're not alone.

What follows is a graphic, candid, honest story of one woman's journey, starting as a child, before, during, and after sexual abuse. Woven throughout my story are poems from myself and other survivors of sexual abuse. If it happened to you, this story is for you. If it happened to someone you love, this story is for you. If you want to help yourself or someone else, this story is for you.

❦

Journal Entry: Mother's Day 2014

Thinking about my own mother today, I wish that I could say we've resolved all our issues and have a beautiful relationship. When I was twenty-five and in intensive therapy, I hoped that after confronting her with the past we'd be able to move comfortably into the future. Instead, she felt that I blamed her for the choices I made that led to my incarceration. She couldn't understand what I desperately needed to express, and I didn't understand why she wouldn't be honest, accept her inability to protect me, and forgive herself as I had forgiven her. Eventually, I stopped seeking her acknowledgment, love, respect, and acceptance.

Today, I don't see my mother very often. She doesn't write to me. She doesn't send money. She doesn't send cards (maybe the rare one for my birthday). At first, I wrote to her often. Then I learned that she didn't always read my letters. I decided long ago that I wasn't going to waste my time and ink writing letters to people who weren't my children and weren't writing back. I know my mother loves me, even though it would seem that she doesn't. When she has visited, she has held me tightly and cried. On the occasions when I phone her, I can't get a word in because she "has so much to tell me."

Recently, another visitor helped me to understand how difficult it can be emotionally for those who live on the outside to visit a prison, to come into contact with a very alien world. It must be even more difficult for my mother, since she probably continues to blame herself, at least in part, for my present situation. Perhaps that's one reason why she visits me so infrequently.

It's taken a lifetime, but I've learned that expressions of love are foreign and difficult for my mother to display to her children. But she tries. She loves me to the best of her ability, and I love her. I used to love her simply because she gave birth to me and I thought I was supposed to. Now I love her in spite of herself, for all that she is, for the good that she's done and the values that she instilled in her three daughters. I wouldn't trade her for the television mothers I used to covet, because she helped to shape me into the woman and mother I have become—a woman I am finally proud of.

❦

I was hesitant to share my memoir until I read an interview with Iyanla Vanzant in *Essence* magazine. She said, "When you tell your story, you free yourself and give other people permission to acknowledge their own story."

I've told mine. Now tell yours. It will free you.

CHAPTER 1

September 2010

"God is with me. God is with me. God is with me."

I stare into the fluorescent lights, much the way I used to stare at the bare bulb by my bed, and repeat this mantra until a sharp pain shoots across my stomach. The pain and cramping bring me back to the present. I glare at the nurse, but she smiles sweetly, says, "How do you feel, honey?" What kind of question is that!

I glance down the length of my body to the white sheet draped casually across my knees. I want to raise my left foot from the stirrups and kick the doctor and his instruments from between my legs. Instead I say, "I'm okay," and grit my teeth through the spasms.

Cancerous cells—how did I get here? Does it matter that I'm a young thirty-eight?

I read somewhere that if you had your first experience of sexual intercourse at a young age, smoked, had HPV or multiple male sex partners (who also had multiple partners), you'd likely be at risk for cervical cancer and precancerous lesions. I should have known. In fact, I think I always did know.

I sigh audibly and try to relax.

God is with me, God is with me, but I remember a time when He wasn't with me, when the light bulb was bare.

My doctor tells me that I will be scheduled for a follow-up Pap smear in six weeks. "Six weeks?" I could already see me driving myself crazy waiting for a follow-up, like when I almost went insane anticipating my HIV results. OMG. The distance between me and the infection control nurse who would give me that news felt like the Green Mile. When he told me it was nonreactive, I wanted to grab strangers and kiss them. I was so happy. I refrained from that activity, though, because freely giving my love is what led to that blood test being needed in the first place. Instead, I vowed, "I will stop being so careless from this moment on."

The past, however, will always catch up and walk closely beside you. Even in my excitement, I wrestled with feelings of disgust over my promiscuous history.

❦

"Don't kiss me, don't touch me excessively, and damn it, don't hold me afterward! Just stick it in, let me hold on to you, and pound me quickly to get it over with. No, I don't want money, your love, or foreplay. I want you to do what men do and get away from me!"

"What's up with you?"

"Nothing!" I swung my feet to the floor and jumped off the bed. "I just don't want any strings or attachments. I don't want a relationship."

He lit a cigarette in the semi-darkness and pulled the sheet up to his waist.

"You act like I asked to be with you or something. I thought we was just fuckin'." He exhaled slowly.

I watched the smoke rise, wishing I could simply dissolve with it into the air. I had been seeing him for four months, and I felt no attraction for him. My anger was spent. What was I doing?

"I didn't like the way you touched my hair. I don't want all of that."

"What do you want?"

I looked at the dull furnishings of the hotel room, similar to all the various hotels I'd been in, and was tempted to tell the truth: Those were the things I wanted but never admitted to myself or anyone else. Instead, I crawled across the bed and took the length of him in my hand. I wanted to please him. His moans excited me, and I was sure I had power and control over him, over all of them.

I gave myself to them willingly, obediently, because I feared them, they chose me, and I had long ago lost the option to say no.

❦

Sheena King

Preyed Upon

The birds once flew and soared so high,
wings extended, heads to the sky,
until the hunters' arrows pluck them
from between the clouds
and we see them tumble.
The ground rushes up to meet them.
What was once a hop in their step
is slowed, by this stabbing pain,
to a sluggish limp. Head down,
pecking at the dirt, crippled,
confused, no longer interested
in seeds that once nourished,
or in the chirping chatter of friends.
Wings close, protectively over breasts,
over slow-beating hearts, unflapping;
the will to fly has vanished, along with
the song from their throats—beaks
sealed shut like windows slammed
against a cold that now encases their hearts.

We hear no songs of dreams,
of joy, of star-filled skies,
of love, of life's comings and goings.
All is silent, instead, in throats swollen
by lumps of unsung pain.

CHAPTER 2

July 1981

"You can't beat me at Old Maid."

"Yes, I can, Jeff! I win at all games!" I yelled in delight as I raced to the shelf where we kept the cards and board games. I was almost nine years old, and Jeff had recently moved into our one-bedroom apartment in Philadelphia as my mother's companion and stepfather to my sisters and me. (In my community, your mother's boyfriend was automatically your stepfather or an "uncle.")

My two younger sisters and I once shared the lone bedroom, but it was no longer ours now and we were sleeping in a small corner of the living room. This arrangement was fine with us, because we were closer to the refrigerator and could curb our frequent attacks of the munchies.

I ran from the dining room and threw the cards on the coffee table. "Prepare to be defeated, Jeff," I said, and shuffled the cards the way Mom had taught me. I wanted her to play with us, but she was out with her sister and some of their friends.

"Shh!" Jeff whispered. "You're going to wake up your sisters."

I looked over at them and smiled. My middle sister had her arm protectively over our baby sister, and I envied their closeness. They were only a year apart, but I was five years older than my middle sister. So Jeff was my friend.

We played until my eyes grew tired.

"Let's play tug-of-war."

"Okay," I said, trying to muster some enthusiasm. I pulled the sheet Jeff brought out with all my strength. I dug my toes into the hardwood floor, but with one quick jerk I landed on Jeff's lap. Hearing my mom's voice in my head, *Don't sit on any man's lap*, I tried to slide off. Jeff held me tightly and whispered, "It's cool, Sheena—we're friends."

"Uh-uh, my mom said I can't."

"It's alright."

"No, it's not," I whined, struggling to get off his lap.

"But, I'm like your daddy."

I felt creepy, and when he mentioned my daddy, I stiffened. He let me go.

"Let's play Crazy Eights," Jeff said, and he sat on the floor after he grabbed the playing cards. I sat down on the floor with the coffee table between us.

"If we met at the playground, would we be friends?"

"I don't know."

"Would we play on the sliding board?"

"Yup, and the swings too. Swings are my favorite thing, Jeff."

"We could be friends, and since I'm a boy, then I could be your boyfriend."

"Yeah," I said, thrilled with the thought of playing on the swings.

This dialogue continued. It was the grooming process, and I was comfortable with Jeff. He was my friend. He listened to me talk endlessly about school, my puppy, and my insane cat, Taboo II. Jeff was my friend.

No one could replace my daddy in my heart, but Jeff was an acceptable substitute. Yes, he was my friend and he liked being around me. I wasn't a burden to him. However, I would soon discover that a man's idea of friendship is entirely different from a nine-year-old girl's.

"I'm finished now. I'm sleepy." I rubbed my eyes and stood up.

"Okay, give me a goodnight hug."

I wrapped my arms around his neck and felt my nightgown rise over my head. Jeff pulled my panties down and ran his big, rough hands all over my body. My mind screamed, *Bad touch!* and my body became rigid in fear. A voice that I hardly recognized squeaked, "I'm tellin' my mommy."

He said, "She's not going to believe you, and she'll beat you for lying."

How was this happening? Jeff was my friend. He cooked for us and told us funny stories about his sisters. He played with us and made Mommy happy. Was this my fault? Mommy said that we weren't to sit on a man's lap because sometimes things happen to a man when a girl sits on his lap. I didn't mean to.

I kept looking at my long white nightgown with little pink flowers on it, wondering why it wasn't on me. I was rooted to this spot, focused on my nightie. I wanted my nightie. I pulled away from Jeff, but he grabbed my arm and pulled me into him.

"I'll kill your simple little ass if you say anything," Jeff hissed in my ear.

I hate to be whispered to, and I haven't liked anyone near my ears since I was five, when my mom's friend, Ms. Stacy, playing at something (I'm still not sure what), said she wanted to whisper to me but stuck her tongue in my ear instead.

"I don't care. I'm telling," I whined.

"Bitch, she's not going to believe your lying ass."

"I'm not lying." I was crying now. Jeff pinched the nipples on my flat chest and rubbed in and around my secret place. My mind went blank. I could think of nothing except his words, "She's not going to believe you." *Jeff is right, isn't he?* She hadn't believed me less than a year before, when I ran from the bathroom into the living room, crying, "He put his hand in my panties and was rubbing my butt." I was running from my father.

I had always been a daddy's girl, and his breakup with my mother pained me. My father was still in love with my mother, so he was a frequent guest at our apartment. I was so hopeful that they'd get back together. When he left at her request, I cried, "Daddy, don't leave me. Take me with you!"

"I can't. You need to be with your mother." I ran to the bathroom with tears streaming down my face. "I want to be left alone!" My dad came into the bathroom, sat on the white wicker hamper, and held me. He tried to calm me down by telling me, "I'll be back next weekend to take you with me."

I cried harder, because I heard my mom say, "Stop telling her that you'll come see her and when you don't, I'm the one who hears her crying! Stop lying to her, Billy!"

My dad hugged me and rubbed my back until his hand traveled too far down. I stopped crying. *This is the bad touch!* I backed away and ran to tell my mommy.

She sent me to my room, but I didn't make it that far. The hallway from the living room to the bedroom was an L shape. I hid at the short part of the L so I could hear.

My mom yelled in anger, although I could hear my dad denying what I said. "Rose, I was only holding her and consoling her while she cried."

After a few minutes of this, it seemed that she accepted his explanation, and he left. I walked dejectedly to my room and cried myself to sleep. My mom didn't come in to talk to me about it or show concern for what I had told her.

My sisters had been staying with my aunt for the weekend, but I really needed them that night. The youngest always made me laugh, and the middle one gave hugs that made me forget why I needed one in the first place.

At breakfast the next morning, I stared into my bowl of oatmeal, wanting my mom to say something about what my daddy had done. But her only response was, "Sheena, eat your cereal before it gets cold." I couldn't raise my head to look at her.

So when Jeff told me, "She's not going to believe you," I knew he spoke the truth. If she believed me, why didn't she cuss my daddy out? Why didn't she hit him like she had done so many times before when he was seeing other women and she was seeing other men? If she believed me, why didn't she hold me and tell me he would never do that again?

I stopped struggling with Jeff and watched my sisters sleeping contentedly. I wanted to be on the bottom bunk between them.

"If you open your mouth, I will kill you and your sisters." This was the first time someone threatened to kill my family and me, but it would not be the last.

When I started to cry again, Jeff picked me up and carried me to my mother's bed. He pulled his penis out of his pants and put my hand on it while he pulled on my nipples and rubbed my ass. When he finished with me, he sent me to the living room. I put my underwear and nightgown back on and squeezed between my sisters instead of climbing up to the top bunk. I didn't want to be alone.

I had just turned nine, and nothing seemed different but nothing was the same. I went to school every day and excelled in all my classes. I signed up for any activities that would keep me in school for longer periods. But this was pointless, because night after night when my mother was out, Jeff would pull and probe with his fingers.

One day his routine changed. "Sit down right there on the bed," he said, pointing to the edge of my mom's bed. I did as he directed and he pulled his penis from the opening in his pants and put it to my lips. "Suck it like taffy." I had a swimming competition in school the following day. This is what I thought about while his hand held my head and his penis filled my mouth.

I started to withdraw inside myself. On my family's game night, I would participate, but my mind would be anywhere but there. "Sheena, what's wrong with you?"

"Nothing, Mom."

Jeff progressed. He took my nightgown off one night and laid me on my back on my mother's bed. He climbed on top of me and rubbed his penis between my legs.

In an attempt to protect itself from horrors that it cannot comprehend, the mind will shut itself down, retreat to safety. As if I had an off switch, I was gone. I had found a safe place inside myself, and I stayed there until hot semen shot up my stomach.

He wiped it off with a washrag and left me sitting there. I got in the tub, in water as hot as I could stand, hoping I would drown, go down the drain, or that my skin would melt off. I could hear Jeff's voice: "You are so pretty. Look at all that long, pretty hair. When you grow some titties, you'll be perfect."

I could see him rubbing butter on my chest because someone told him it makes your breasts grow. I scrubbed my body, wanting to scream but afraid of frightening my sisters. I could hear them laughing and playing with Jeff. *What if he does that to them? I have to tell my mommy. I can't let him hurt my sisters. Mommy said we have to protect each other.*

That night my mom was loud and silly from Southern Comfort and weed when she came home, so I woke up. I was determined to tell her. "Mommy . . ."

"Sheena, take your ass to sleep. What're you doin' up? You have school tomorrow!"

My mother's quick temper was legendary, and the punishments were always severe. I did as I was told.

I don't understand a man's attraction for a child, but it must have been intense, because Jeff grew bolder. Soon he no longer limited his violations to the quiet of the night. Whenever my mom was out of the house, day or night, for hours or just briefly, Jeff would take me to my mother's room. I stopped wearing nightgowns and would only wear pajamas and wrap myself tightly in my blanket. Somehow, I thought this would protect me.

Sheena King

Wounded

You have sown.
What will you reap?

Pain twisted, buried inside.
A dark moving mass of hate-filled love
that cripples and confuses.
Bodies too young to take
this blow dealt by fate.
Covered faces mask smiles
that distort features but
never touch their eyes.

What have you sown?

A wall of resolve,
facade of feigned bravery,
drugs, drinks, violence,
sex slavery.
A life that might have been truth,
your perversion turns into a lie.
Inhale, exhale, they
move forward, yet stand still…

You *will* reap!

Do not blame her when she descends,
headlong and with abandon
into the pit. She is pushed by your hand,
the one that touches, probes young flesh.

Warped affections.
Here is a child for you to molest.

What will you reap?

Minds too young and innocent,
unequipped to comprehend adult desire.
Should she tell someone? Who will help her?
She does not tell; no one can defend her.
Left, then, with violations and scars
from cuts so deep:
a profusion of blood that flows
freely from unhealed wounds.

Molesters beware.
What you have sown,
this, also, will you reap.

CHAPTER 3

September 1981

If there was any place where I felt safe and sought solace, it was in the classroom. I was a loner, and that wasn't a problem for anyone when I sat behind my desk at Pickett Middle School. I wouldn't raise my hand, because I didn't want to draw attention to myself and if I spoke too quickly, I had a tendency to stutter. (My mother said that my mind was running faster than my mouth could.) But when I was called on to answer a question, I was never wrong.

I was in the fifth grade, and I took schooling very seriously. That was the one thing my mother loved to brag about me: "Sheena is very smart." I was the one to place my pencil down on the desk first. My classroom assignments were completed quickly and effortlessly.

Days turned to months, and fifth grade progressed to sixth grade. Children being true to themselves, the teasing began: "Sheena's a bookworm. She thinks she's smarter than everyone else."

I didn't like to be teased, nor did I appreciate the unwanted attention. I never sat in the front row unless I was assigned that seat. I didn't talk in class. I preferred to remain in the background, to be invisible. When the teasing started, I held my pencil in my left hand a little longer and pretended that I was still working, struggling over an answer until several of my classmates were done. This didn't appease my tormenters.

One day a girl who sat behind me made a huge error in judgment. I ignored her taunts: "Smarty-pants, bookworm, that's why you don't have any friends." Maybe she was upset that I ignored her. I was used to ignoring words that stung. No one else's words could compare to my mother's. This girl threw her pencil at me and clunked me in the back of my head.

Quietly, over my shoulder, I said, "See you after school."

I did, on Chelten Avenue behind JC Penney. I beat her until my cousin Nicky pulled me off. And I was still trying to go after her. Once I came back to myself, I could finally see my cousin and hear her say, "Sheena, no—that's enough." It took me a few minutes to gain my bearings. All I saw was red. I thought my mother would see red when she found out I was suspended. However, in her mind it was acceptable to be suspended for fighting, because protecting yourself was something she endorsed. Honestly, it had been forced on me.

In elementary school, my CAT scores were so high my teachers, with my mother's permission, scheduled me for the "mentally gifted" test. Those scores were also high, and my mother asked me if I wanted to enroll in Masterman, a school for gifted children, after detailing the type of school it was. "No," I said, "because I'll just be one of the smart kids in that school instead of the smartest kid in the school."

It was cool to be smart in elementary school, until I was bused from Emlen, in Germantown, to a school that was predominantly white. There was one other African American girl on the bus, Lisa, and I had the misfortune of sitting next to her because I was the last one to be picked up. She pulled my hair, gave me "Indian burns" or "frogs" on my right arm. I couldn't take it anymore. After three days of this, I told my mother.

"Sheena, you'd better beat her ass before I beat yours! If you come in here tomorrow with another mark from this girl, I'm fucking you up!" The last thing I wanted was a beating from my mother.

Lisa pulled my hair again. She pulled my long braids so viciously I yelped in pain. Later, as we were about to walk through the glass doors on the second floor of our school, I grabbed her by her short ponytails and slammed her head into the brass door handles. She didn't bother me again, and I happily reported this event to my mother. She was proud of me. This was what she had meant when she told us to always protect ourselves. I didn't yet know how to protect myself against adults. I thought that was her job. But I was fueled with enough anger to protect myself against my peers, to protect my sisters, and to protect anyone who was being bullied or taken advantage of. And so it began.

❦

I didn't feel that I fit or belonged anywhere, and I retreated further and further inside myself. I couldn't understand why God would let this happen to me. I stopped praying. I hated God and I hated myself.

When Jeff would finish with me, I would pull my hair out by the handfuls, and it would stop the hurt I felt inside. When I wanted to scream but didn't want to wake my little sisters or anger my mother, I'd dig my fingernails into my thighs or bang my head on the wall. This seemed to make the screams inside of me go silent.

A fire started in the basement. My cat woke my mom by jumping on her face. Because of the fire, we found ourselves living in a shelter. I was embarrassed and hated it, but at least Jeff couldn't be there, because it was a shelter for women and children. I had a difficult time sleeping, and late one night after we had been in the shelter for a couple of weeks, I thought I heard someone calling me. I looked out the window and was paralyzed with fear. There was Jeff outside my window, gesturing for me to open it.

The window opened inward, and we usually kept it open to catch a breeze. My sisters and I were in one room while my mom was next door. Our small room had two beds, one for me and one for my sisters to share. There was a square cut in the wall so our mother could see us. I screamed through that square, "Mom, Jeff's out there!"

I saw what I thought was disappointment shadowing his face. I didn't care. He climbed in through her window, and I slid in the small bed between my sisters with an arm around both of them—to feel safe myself and to protect them.

I don't know how I survived on a few hours of restless sleep each night, but I managed to present one face to the world while I sought solace in a dark place that I created inside myself. I was incompetent at making friends because I seemed odd to myself. I felt different. I couldn't understand girls my age. They were worried about boys, the latest dance steps, clothes, and crushes on teachers, while I worried whether Jeff was going to climb in my window and steal me in the middle of the night.

I thought every man was a monster, a molester, and every father touched his daughter and everyone knew what was happening to me but no one cared. I was dirty, a failure. I hated my body and myself. I fought many boys, even those who tried to befriend me. But I had no idea why. I would become intensely angry with little or no provocation, and the only way I could successfully rid myself of the anger was physical harm to my body or to someone else's.

Often I was suspended from school for fighting. Once, the guidance counselor suggested to my mother that she seek a psychiatrist for me before I returned to school. But this never happened. My father's mother and his brothers and sister would often ask me if I was alright. They noticed the changes: I didn't laugh as much (and I loved to laugh). I would stare at nothing for long stretches of time, or stiffen when I was hugged. They may have wondered why I refused to wear nightgowns and sleep alone. I insisted that I sleep with my grandmother.

"Na-Na, what's the matter?"

I smiled. "Nothing, Auntie Cheryl."

"Are you sure? You know you can talk to me."

"I know. I'm gonna go play on my computer." I ran up the steps and stared out of the window instead, wondering if I should have told.

I loved spending weekends with my paternal grandmother, Mom-Mom. She spoiled me and we had so much fun. I was especially close to my Uncle Pete and secretly wished he were my father instead of my father's brother. He was a practical joker and would pinch my nose every time I'd see him. I pulled away from him one day, and he gave me a long, searching look. "Na, if somebody is touching you, you can tell me."

"Huh?"

My uncle usually got right to the point, and many people feared him because he was no-nonsense and very skilled with his hands. "Is that pussy Jeff doing things to you? You can tell me, and he'll never do it again!"

I could sense the fury boiling beneath the surface. "No … no, Uncle Petie."

I hated lying to my family, especially my uncle, because I could tell him anything and I knew he'd protect me. My uncle's heavy gaze seemed to bore right through me, and for a moment his handsome face was distorted by emotions that I couldn't name, so I lowered my eyes to the floor. I fought the urge to speak the truth, because the last time I told my family something like this—how my mother's husband, Tee (the one after my father), had brutally beaten me and my sisters—my mother punished me by forbidding me to go to my grandmother's house for several months.

I remembered how, when I was seven, I packed my suitcase and snuck out before anyone was awake, riding three buses to my maternal grandmother's house. "What are you doing here, girl?" Nana asked. In a flurry of words and self-righteous anger, I told her, "Last night Tee held me upside down by my leg and beat me with a belt, and then he made me go to bed without dinner, so I … I left!"

Nana told me to go sit in the living room and turn on the cartoons while she made me breakfast. I obliged. I love breakfast! Keenly observant or even nosy, I watched television and enjoyed the smells of eggs, sausage, grits, and toast while listening in abject fear as my grandmother recounted everything I had just told her. I knew she was talking to my mother and that Mom was going to kill me. When she put up a tray and placed the steaming plate in front of me, I was no longer interested in food. "Why'd you tell her?"

"She's your mother."

"But she's your daughter! Tell her not to beat me!"

"Sheena, she's my daughter, but she is your mother and I can't tell her how to raise you. Now eat up, your mom's coming to get you. She was worried about you."

"You're making me leave?"

Nana sat down next to me and rubbed my head. "Your mother wants you with her."

I looked at this little Indian woman with incredibly long, wavy hair and soft skin creased with age. I touched what I thought was a wrinkle in her cheek. In reality, it was a scar from a straight razor. I said with terror and sincerity, "Your daughter's gonna kill me. She told me what happens in the house stays in the house."

She laughed without teeth—they were in a jar on the back of the toilet—and said, "Now eat up."

I wanted to eat the sausage at least, but I had lost my appetite. When my mom arrived, she didn't kill me. But I wished she had.

Journal Entry: August 1, 1998

It's 4:30 a.m. and I've been awake for an hour remembering. I'm angry because I don't want to remember but I do. I want to sleep but I can't. My eyes are so tired but my heart is racing. I remember not wanting him to fuck me. I remember being afraid and crying. I think he's the reason that I can't sleep on my back except for a few minutes (maybe thirty at the most) without waking up with my heart racing. I always looked back and figured that I wanted him to do it, because sometimes it felt good. I never wanted him to do it, and I never knew the body was supposed to respond to sexual stimuli. I never wanted him to do it! I didn't entice him. I was a kid and I'm remembering. I remember staring at the light bulb for hours at a time. Mom would ask me what I was doing, and I would say, "Thinking." I caught myself doing that the other day. I can get lost staring at a bulb and I never know what I'm thinking. I think I just space out. I remember not wanting to wear a nightgown, only shorts and T-shirts to bed. I wouldn't wear bikinis or lacy underwear until I came to jail. I hadn't slept alone and naked until I was in jail in a single cell. Why are these memories flooding back now? Is it because I've been wondering about who/what this "inner child" is? I'll have to read up and learn about that. I think I protect her, because I'm often holding myself tightly in a fetal position, like a few minutes ago when I couldn't turn my mind off. I don't remember ever hating her but I must have, because I've done and allowed other things to be done to me.

CHAPTER 4

December 1982

There were so many reasons to feel discontent and so little to be happy about. Children need consistency, and there was none. We didn't stay in any apartment long enough to establish a routine.

I wasn't in a school long enough to make friends, but I longed for them. I wasn't an outcast. There were a few neighbors, classmates, and teammates who would speak to me. I simply felt that I didn't belong or couldn't relate, and my personal shame prevented me from having close ties to anyone. Living in a shelter worsened my situation. I was embarrassed that we didn't have a home of our own. I remember the first shelter. It resembled a tall, narrow haunted house. It was gloomy and quiet. We shared one room with two beds, and we weren't allowed to have our own food. My mom would sneak in small cans of potted meat, Vienna sausages, and saltine crackers. We ate so much of it that now I can't stand the sight of Vienna sausages or potted meat!

The residents of this shelter were elderly, and no one spoke to us. My sisters were afraid, and each day my familiar anger grew. Until I was twenty-five, anger was the only emotion that I knew, was comfortable with, and was capable of expressing—in a variety of ways.

We left this shelter after I became violently ill from drinking spoiled milk in the soggy cereal the staff called breakfast. My mother was protective of outsiders hurting us, and her legendary temper had us seeking shelter once again. Finally, she found a place for women and children.

One would think that I could easily have made friends there because we had homelessness in common, but that was not the case. After school and homework, I would play with my sisters, run errands to the cheesesteak shop on Stenton Avenue, or explore the grounds. We were permitted to have our own food, and my grandmother lived just a few blocks from us. Unfortunately, there must have been an unlimited supply of outdated milk, because this shelter also served it for breakfast.

I did enjoy my exploration of the grounds. They were expansive and perfect for my overactive imagination. I love nature, and this place had beautiful flowers, trees, and grassy areas. There was also a playground. I would watch the swings move slowly from the wind and imagine children who had lived there before me swinging on them and laughing loudly. At times my thoughts would turn dark and I would imagine that the swings were moving from the ghosts of children who had been murdered at this shelter and whose bodies were buried in the sizable backyard.

Following the lead of one of my cousins, in school I enrolled in a dance class. For an auditorium performance, the instructor placed me in the front, but during the performance I danced my way to the back. I have never felt comfortable in front of a crowd. I still don't. Although in recent years I have forced myself to stand in front of crowds, I am not comfortable and I may never be. Still, in order to grow, I have to come out of my comfort zone, or I risk remaining stuck in the past, haunted by nightmares and plagued by what-ifs. So, comfortable or not, I try to push myself.

However, I wasn't ready for the push when I was eleven, even with activities that brought me comfort and contentment, like swimming.

I knew that I was fast and could do every stroke with unmatched accuracy. But when I sensed the envy from others on my team, I would purposely make a mistake in order to be sent back to the beginning. The same way I would pretend in the classroom, I began to pretend in the pool. I didn't want to incite jealousy. I wanted friends. Coupled with the conflict of being an overachiever, but trying not to be, was my sexual confusion. After swimming practice, we would shower and blow-dry our hair in the locker room. I would wait until last, because I was ashamed to expose a body that an adult male stole pleasure from.

I was also ashamed of my attraction to girls. My mother said it was wrong, an abomination before God, when she caught me and a neighbor my age, two years prior. She proceeded to beat "the devil" out of me. As for Lil, the neighbor, for several years after that day I was convinced my mom had killed her, because I didn't see her again until we were both sixteen, pushing our first children in strollers.

❦

One of the places we landed after we left the second shelter was the Richard Allen housing projects. I was eager to live there, because I wanted the opportunity to invite people over after school as I had seen others do. One day I was invited to Lamar's house after school. He pushed me onto his bed to kiss and dry-hump me. I went ballistic, so that never happened with him again—especially after I beat up his cousin, the girl who had hit me in the back of my head in class with her pencil.

Once we arrived in the projects, Jeff moved in and picked up where he had left off. He pinched and pulled on my nipples again. He was back to sliding his penis between my legs and leaving semen on my stomach. He continued to convince my young, trusting mind that my mom would be mad at me.

Before long, he added a new twist. "Your sisters are getting big," he said, and licked his lips.

"Don't talk about my sisters!" This conversation didn't feel right, and I was getting angry.

"Yeah, they look so pretty."

I could feel the tears coming. "Don't touch my sisters, please." I couldn't fathom allowing these things to happen to them. I was their protector, the big sister. "Leave them alone!"

Jeff laughed. "If you tell anybody anything, they'll be my girlfriends too."

❦

I stared at the red, dripping lines on my right forearm. I felt a little bit better. The pain in my stomach and pressure in my head were gone—just like that. This was faster than pulling out my hair, digging my nails in my thighs, or banging my head on the wall.

I washed the steak knife with Dawn dish detergent, put it on the drain board, and rinsed the blood off my arm. The cuts weren't deep, more like scratches, but they served the purpose.

❦

I looked at the ceiling for cracks that were made visible by the lights on Tenth Street. I could usually envision cartoon images that would entertain me. I heard, more than saw, Jeff opening my bedroom door. I squeezed my eyes and held tightly to my blue blanket. I pretended to be asleep, although it didn't matter to him. He lifted me effortlessly from my bed, through the short hall to my mother's bedroom.

I tried to find cracks in the ceiling to squeeze myself into. I found one and took my mind to that safe place. Then I was unexpectedly grabbed and yanked out of it. *What is he doing to me?!* I felt a cold wetness. I opened my eyes, looked down the length of my body, and was appalled. Jeff was leaving a trail of slimy saliva from my neck down my chest and stomach and in between my thighs. *Oh my God, please help me! Why is he doing that?*

I felt like filth, and I couldn't find my crack in the ceiling. I had to shut down. This wasn't a conscious act. Some part of me automatically shut off like a light switch. I don't remember when or how I returned to my own bed.

I spent the next week in a dreamlike state, moving from moment to moment on autopilot, not caring about the menstrual cramps. They were, in fact, a blessing, because Jeff kept his distance.

When he wasn't violating me, he tried to be friends. "Na, I made cheesesteaks and cheese fries, come eat."

My mom seemed to favor men who were employed sporadically, doing odd jobs or nothing at all except loafing around the house while she worked two and three jobs. Every man that was ever in her life since my birth could cook, though, which was a plus because she was not good at it.

"I'm going outside." My mother had to force me to go out

because I was painfully shy. I also believed that everyone knew, or strongly suspected, what was happening to me. Later, that would prove to be prophetic, at least with regard to people outside my immediate family.

"You're not going anywhere. Sit down and eat!"

I grabbed my rope, intending to find someone to jump double Dutch with.

"Sit the fuck down."

"You're not my father. You don't tell me what to do!" I yelled, wondering where that had come from.

"Oh yeah?" sneered Jeffrey. "And where is he at, huh?"

I exhaled loudly and sat down at the opposite end of the table. "Where are my sisters?"

"They already ate. They're outside playing."

My throat tightened. Whenever he planned to do things to me during the day, he'd send my sisters outside. There was a black plastic canister with a gray top about two inches tall and one inch in diameter on the table in front of my plate. I had seen a container like this before. My mom put her marijuana seeds inside one. I never liked the effects of marijuana, but my mother was from a not-so-unusual school of thought that believed if she allowed us to do certain things in the house, we'd be less inclined to do them in the streets. So she smoked her weed with us, whether we wanted to or not.

My mom was a screamer and quite vicious with the things she said when her ferocious temper got the best of her. Her words ripped me apart, and they had shattered the little self-esteem I had. I was a master, therefore, at tuning people out when they were talking. Occasionally, however, a few snatches of Jeff's monologue found their way through my protective barrier. He was saying something about what would happen when I got a boyfriend.

The problem with blocking people out is that you may miss something important or interesting. I stared at his curly hair, trying to focus. I couldn't look in his handsome face, because I hated to peer into the eyes that stared at me like my blossoming body was a shrimp and steak dinner, nor could I look at the lips that were speaking, because I didn't want to think about the atrocious things he did to me with them. I hoped he was saying that he'd leave me alone when I got a boyfriend. I resolved to find one today. There was no shortage of boys who thought I was pretty or made comments about my butt. Unfortunately, he wasn't saying anything remotely close to that.

"... he's going to be smaller than I am."

"What?" I interrupted.

He took a huge bite before putting his steak sandwich down. He grabbed a napkin and wiped ketchup and strings of cheese from his mustache before continuing. "You wasn't listening?"

"No."

I pushed my French fries around the plate with my fingers, making designs through the ketchup. I scraped some Hellmann's off the roll and added it to my ketchup design. Jeff watched this for a few seconds and then asked with what seemed like genuine concern, "Sheena, what's the matter?"

My mind screamed, *You're the matter, pussy! The shit you do to me is the matter! That I cut on myself to stop the hurt and stop my mind from racing is the matter, you roach!*

Instead, I continued to push my fry around the plate like I was creating a masterpiece. I couldn't be bothered with his trivial question.

"You can talk to me, Na-Na. You know I love you."

Love? That's love? My dad loves me too. My mom says she loves my sisters and me after she smokes a joint, but she beats us for sport, yells, and screams at us from the minute she gets in from work until she goes to sleep. Love? If this is love, I don't ever want it from anybody.

My facial expression must have betrayed my thoughts, because he reiterated, "I do love you. And like I was saying, when you get a boyfriend his dick is going to be smaller than mine, so you have to learn to tighten yourself down there."

What? Tighten what? I didn't know what he was talking about. I was eleven, about to turn twelve in five months. My mom had already given me "the talk" and assured me that when I was "ready" to let her know so she could take me to get birth control pills and condoms. I paid attention in hygiene class, but he never put it in that way, so what was I supposed to "tighten down there"?

I was confused and started to play with the heart pendant on my chain. I traced my finger over my initials, which were engraved into it. I had received it and matching earrings from my mom on Valentine's Day. Her "love" was always material. The heart was a source of comfort and focus for me. (Years later, it would be a gold cross.) There were no hugs, kisses, "good nights," "good mornings," or sober "I love you's" in my home, but there were gifts. I guess that was love, like this plate of cheesesteak and fries.

My eyes glazed over. I left the table. My body was there, but I wasn't. I couldn't deal with whatever Jeff was implying.

Sniff. Sniff.

I don't know how long I was in my protective shell. I never knew. I blinked several times to clear my vision and saw Jeff sniffing a powdery substance from a straw that had an angled tip. I may not have come from this environment, but I was in North Philly now and I knew exactly what that was—a drug! *I have to get out of here!* I promptly pushed my chair back from the table and went to my room to grab a pair of Nikes. But before I could unlock the front door, Jeff said, "Where are you going? You're on punishment. Do I need to call Rose?"

Damn. I was on punishment for writing what my mother called "hate mail." Periodically, I'd write anonymous notes and leave them in visible places. They would say things like, "I hate you. I hope a Mack truck hits you," or, "I stepped on a crack to break your back." The latest one must have hurt her, because she said, "Stupid ass, I know you're the one writing this hate mail, so cut it the fuck out before I break *your* back." Many, many years later, I read that when children are abused, they try to tell someone in many ways when they can't do it verbally.

I had been grounded for a week. Normally I wouldn't care, since I was frightened in social settings. But it was summer and I loved to swim. I found peace in the water, and when I needed an escape, the playground at night was ideal. It was basically deserted, and if there was too much of a chill in the air, I'd sit on a bench alone with no other company except the trees. Nature soothed me before I found other things that were almost as effective.

I released the doorknob and went out on the balcony.

"No, that's outside. Your mother said you were to stay indoors." His eyes were wide as he wiped powder off his nose and held the container out to me.

I was horrified. "No!"

I turned my back to him and switched the television on, pointedly ignoring him. He was not going to force me to do that as he had forced me to smoke a joint that had made me dizzy, sweaty, and nauseated after one puff. That was the first time I held on to the toilet for dear life. He thought it was funny when he casually mentioned that it was laced with angel dust. On that occasion, he threatened to tell my mother that he had found the drug in my room if I told on him. I didn't even have to conjure up images of beatings with switches cut from the bushes outside, extension cords, her fists, or a thick leather belt that had "Mom's Strap" written on it. The images burned in my mind, because they were daily occurrences for one offense or another. My lips were split so often for saying things she didn't want to hear that I swore it was the cause of them being full and plump. Briefly, I thought about running away again, but each road led right back to Rose. So what was the point?

I closed the door that led to the balcony, kicked off my sneakers, and plopped down on the couch after turning up the TV, attempting to drown out the snorting sounds, the acrid smell of weed, and the scary way Jeff stared at my legs.

"Your legs are so nice." His voice sounded preoccupied, but his eyes were large, round orbs straining to pop out of his head. It was hot, but I didn't care. Normally, I hate to be hot and prefer the month of my birth—December. I went to my room and put on baggy jeans to prevent him from staring at me. As a child, I thought clothes could protect me.

I switched on the light in my room, although it was early afternoon, and turned the lock in the knob. The bare bulb had me transfixed. I wondered if I could go blind by staring at it. Then I wouldn't have to see the way Jeff and other men were looking at me. I've seen men stare at my mother the same way. On one such occasion, when she smiled at their whistling and sexual innuendo, I mumbled, "Whore." I didn't think she heard me, but when we arrived at Mom-Mom's house, my mom took her sister upstairs. My aunt thundered down the steps and said, "Sheena, you called my sister a whore?"

I was sitting on the carpet in front of the floor-model television, leaning against a thick glass-and-chrome coffee table, watching boxing. I ignored her, because I didn't want to lie. She picked me up by my collar, pulled me up the steps to my grandmother's bedroom, and beat me with one of my Mom-Mom's leather belts.

I went back in front of the television, listening to the sobs from my mother, who sat on the love seat. I whispered, "You're still a whore." To my young mind, it was whorish to attract men and bask in their attention.

Later that night, when I sat in the dining room with my grandmother, she gave me one of her hearty laughs in agreement with something I had said. Her booming laughter made me smile. She was the only one who could. I had stopped smiling, but no one in my mother's house seemed to notice. My grandmother had, and she tried to bring smiles back into my life.

I recognize now that I could have told her and she would have believed and defended me, but I didn't know it then. I knew my mother, and I knew not to go up against her.

Sheena King

Haiku

There are a thousand
puzzle pieces on the ground.
It is me—broken.

Vonique Howard

I'll Never Tell

I'll never tell what you did
How you stole my innocence when I was a kid
I'll never tell how you lied
To keep my tears bottled deep inside
I'll never tell what you said
To make me wish, every day, that I was dead
I'll never tell how you smiled
At the age of fourteen, I had your child
I'll never tell of the vicious assault
Making me feel that it was somehow my fault
I'll never tell of the violence too
How you traded my fear for sex with you
I'll never tell how you made me sick
Emotionally, spiritually, and physically—take your pick!
I'll never tell how you pulled that knife
When I finally found the courage to take back my life
I'll never tell for thirty-eight years
My heart screams aloud, and no one hears
But I can't keep silent, not one more day
Because with my daughter you've had your way
Now I want to tell, in any way I can
If it will keep one victim out of your hands
A device to prevent sexual assault, that would surely sell:
Until that invention comes along, I'll always tell

CHAPTER 5

May 1983

I lived with my grandmother for a few months, but I missed my sisters and worried about their safety. My grandmother couldn't take them too, so I returned home and returned to my misery.

I stared into the light bulb, thinking about that misery, when Jeff came crashing through the flimsy door.

"Smoke this."

It smelled different. I slid to the far corner of the mattress. "What is that?"

"It's a joint."

"I don't like weed, Jeff."

"Smoke it anyway."

He loomed over me with his right hand extended, the joint burning brightly. I wouldn't take it. He roughly grabbed my face, blew smoke in my nostrils and partially opened mouth. He had the lit end of it in his mouth. It smelled off, and I felt calm but jittery. I felt as if I was floating on a cloud. He must have put that powder in it that he later told my mom he bought to sell: cocaine.

I don't remember him undressing me. He was on the floor, lying on his back, holding me on top of him with his dirty fingernails digging into my waist. He slid the secret part of me back and forth along the length of his penis. Repulsive. I hated this body that was created to respond. My body had betrayed me, and I hated it and I hated myself. I hated Jeff. I hated men, and I hated my mother for not being enough for him so that he had to take it out on me. I didn't know that his twisted desires had nothing to do with her, or even with me, for that matter. Therefore, I hated, and the rage consumed me. It burned bright red and pulled me from my body. *Pop!* It probably wasn't audible, but it felt like something had popped inside me. Then there was a burning pain and darkness.

That was the first time I welcomed the darkness.

When the light found me, I was in a tub of tepid water. I sat up gasping. I added hot water to the half-filled tub, making it as hot as I could tolerate.

How the hell did I get in the tub? I shouldn't have asked, because the answer came to me in a flood of images. I had lost my virginity to my stepfather, and now I'd never know what it was supposed to be like with your first boyfriend. I scrubbed my body with the back brush until it stung.

I went to bed without dinner. I didn't talk to anyone, not even my sisters. When the apartment was quiet and everyone was asleep, I tiptoed to the living room, which also served as a dining room, as the table was against the wall that separated the living room from the kitchen. I knew Jeff and my mother to be careless, and they did not fail me. The black container with the gray top was still on the table like a centerpiece or a floral arrangement.

I went to the kitchen, opened the top drawer by the sink, and removed a plastic straw. I cut the tip on an angle, like the one Jeff used. I sat at the table in the same chair that I had used earlier. I popped the top off the container, put the cut end of the straw inside it, and scooped up a little of the whitish, powdery substance. I inhaled it, reinserted the straw, and inhaled more in the other nostril.

I didn't care anymore. I didn't care what happened to me. I wanted to float away and never come back. My nose burned, and there was an aspirin taste in the back of my throat. I took the black container with me to the bathroom, dumped the cocaine in the toilet, and flushed with satisfaction. I buried the container under some garbage in the trash can and returned to my room.

I stayed awake that night staring out the window, trying to muster up the courage to jump.

My mother came from shopping not many days later and ceremoniously dropped the bags on the couch.

"Sheena, come look at your clothes."

I looked at them without interest or enthusiasm. "I didn't want dresses, skirts, and shoes. I wanted jeans and sneakers."

"You ungrateful bitch! You are never satisfied! Take this shit to your room and put it away!"

She pushed the bags and shoeboxes toward me and continued her rant about my ingratitude. I walked back to my room, pondering what I was supposed to be grateful about. Should I be grateful for the things that go bump in the night?

"Go the fuck outside!"

"I'm on punishment for cutting class."

I didn't want to go out there. As strange as it seemed, I wanted to be with my mom. Things were confused in my mind.

"I'm tired of you walking around looking crazy and lying every time I ask what's wrong with you."

"You don't really want to know!"

I didn't have to speculate about how she would respond—as usual my lip was cut. I glared at her and sucked the blood from my bottom lip.

"Get the fuck out my face. Keep sitting under me in my damn business!"

I went to my room, put on a one-piece, a pair of cut-off light-blue Guess jeans, a Smurf T-shirt, blue Nikes, and no socks. I lived on Tenth Street and the playground was on Ninth and Brown Streets. I dove in the pool and backstroked under the hot midday sun. I swam until the pool closed that night, but I stayed in the playground. Once the gate surrounding the pool was locked for the night, I climbed over the gate and dove in again. They couldn't keep me out if they wanted to. Peace.

It was short lived. Once he had robbed me of my innocence, Jeff's appetite was insatiable, and my hatred was growing. I began staying outside past my 10 p.m. curfew. I didn't want to be in the house anymore. Sometimes, I would just sit on the step and daydream about what my life could have been with a different set of parents. I wanted the parents I saw on television.

I wouldn't venture farther than the playground. I didn't need to go anywhere else, because the gentle swaying of the leaves in the trees would calm me. I wasn't afraid of what lurked in the streets at night. I was afraid of what preyed on me in the false security of my home.

As usual, my mother misunderstood my actions.

"Why are you hanging out all night in the streets?" She started singing the chorus from a rap: "Project ho, project ho."

That hurt my feelings, and I tried to explain that I enjoyed sitting near the trees. She was already aware that I loved to swim. I had been on swim, track, and gymnastics teams in school.

But those activities had ceased after I'd moved from my grandmother's back to my mother's apartment, because I had to transfer schools. The junior high school in my neighborhood, Stoddart Fleisher, didn't offer any of the extracurriculars that were available at Pickett Middle School in my grandmother's middle-class neighborhood.

I could swim from the time I was six months old. I had always been a natural in the water, but no one from my family attended the meets where I competed. Still, in Pickett, classwork and after-school activities had served as a distraction from all the memories of what was happening to me at home. I don't think I believed I could excel at anything. What didn't come naturally simply didn't come at all, so I didn't put any effort into anything. I wasn't seeking approval. I wanted an escape.

I didn't feel disappointed when my family neglected to attend my competitions, because I felt as if I was the disappointment. My mother and sisters were, however, in attendance at one gymnastics exhibition. My assignment was the balance beam. My execution was flawless, and my mom did say some nice things to me about my performance. But after that night, I refused to advance beyond the balance beam to the parallel bars, because I had also heard her heaping praise on my teammate, Penelope, who had performed on the bars in the exhibition. To my ten-year-old ears, it seemed as if she was prouder of someone else's daughter than she was of her own.

For several weeks following that exhibition, I would purposely make mistakes so I would be sent back to the floor exercises. I repeatedly followed the same pattern: up to the balance beam, then back down to floor exercises. Finally, my instructor informed my mother that I lacked motivation. When she questioned me about my lack of enthusiasm, I said, "I just don't like it anymore."

I regret that now. To this day, I will do a cartwheel when no one's looking and I'll tiptoe on any curb and pretend it's a balance beam. I don't fool myself into believing that I could have been an Olympian like Dominique Dawes or Gabby Douglas, but my lack of self-esteem and confidence prevented me from trying, from believing that I could have been anyone or anything at all.

I made a different kind of mistake on the track team, because it wasn't deliberate. I knew I was fast. I didn't believe I could beat anyone, but my coach believed in me just as much as my swimming instructor did, or my dance teacher, who was always encouraging and never again allowed me to disappear into the back row during a performance. The problem was, I didn't believe in myself, and there wasn't enough positive reinforcement to encourage me to believe.

On one rare occasion, my family attended a race. There were four of us ranging from first to fourth grade, hand-picked by our coaches from four different schools. I was in the second grade, and prepared to fly! With my right foot behind the starting line and my left foot on the block, I turned to my right to smile at my family. When I turned my head back to look at the finish line, determined to make them proud, I heard a woman in the bleachers yell, "Her toe is over the line!"

She couldn't have been talking about me, because I had already checked my running form and the position of my Nikes, I thought. But I always believed in honesty and fair play, so I moved my foot back farther just as the gun sounded. That was a mistake, because I wasn't ready. I took off a beat behind the others and came in second.

I was distraught, but I won't ever forget that day. My mom was so happy. She waved my second-place ribbon in the air like she'd won a million dollars. She still has that ribbon proudly displayed with the trophies and awards won years later by my own children.

As it turned out, the woman who yelled about a toe over the line wasn't talking about me, but about the girl who won first place. She was the fourth grader, a girl I had previously beaten in a different race. (And the woman continued ranting long after the gun sounded and the event was finished.)

For all the things my mother wasn't, there's one thing she was: a woman who instilled values, morals, an appreciation of hard work, and a sense of justice in her children. She understood why I had shifted my foot. On that day, she was actually proud of me, and she rewarded me with my favorite cookies: oatmeal raisin.

Racing was great, but swimming was my serenity. And thus there was more than one time as I was growing up when I climbed over the locked gate of a swimming pool and dove in.

Sheena King

I know, but you don't

You don't know the things I've been through
the dark valley of life I've sojourned from, and to.
You don't know why I cry when I'm alone.
You don't know the hell that I call home.
You don't know.

You don't know the tragedies, the trauma.
You don't know my misery, the drama.
You don't know the ache my smile covers.
You don't know the debauchery of my lovers.
You don't know.

You don't know the depth of my confusion.
You don't know my secrets, my delusions.

You don't know the family of my curse.
You don't know my unwanted birth.
You don't know.

You don't know the light that permeates,
the perplexities of a soul who waits,
while watching for this life to pass,
for the pain to end in a peaceful death—
at last.

You don't know.

CHAPTER 6

August 1983

My mother continued to call me a whore. "Ho, since you can't seem to get in at your curfew, you're on punishment for two weeks. You will not go out of this house for anything."

That lasted four days. "I'm sick of seeing your sickening, stupid ass walking back and forth looking at the floor!"

What she didn't see was that I was pacing back and forth trying to find a way to tell her what Jeff was doing.

I also wanted her to know that my middle sister was doing weird things like drinking Clorox bleach but wouldn't tell me why. I asked her if Jeff was bothering her, but she said he wasn't, and from the look she gave me, I had to acknowledge that there was no lie in her hazel eyes. I was too young to understand what it meant, if it meant anything at all, or if it was normal. I didn't understand what normal was either. Maybe that's what a seven-year-old middle child does.

I pushed myself to tell my mother about it, because I had long ago stopped caring about myself but it was my duty to protect my sisters. She cussed her out, made her cry, but failed to find out what was behind her actions.

Looking at my sister's pretty eyes turn blue because she was sad broke my heart. Something was wrong, but what?

"Sheena, why are you still here? Go play."

"Mom, I don't have anybody to play with."

My mother threw open the balcony door and hollered down to a couple of preteen girls who were untangling a plastic-coated line for jumping rope.

"Do y'all need another person?"

"Yes," the two girls answered.

"Do you want her to play?" she shouted, pointing in my direction.

"Yeah," the tallest one answered.

"See? Now go," my mother said, pushing me back inside the apartment.

I hoped she would talk to my sister while I was outside. Later I found out that she hadn't. I grabbed my shell tops and ran down the four flights of steps. I made friends! I started going out every day to jump double Dutch—until my mother was hired full-time at the IRS. I guess working 11 p.m. until 7 a.m. at Mellon Bank wasn't enough.

Things at home changed once again. My friends would come to get me, but Jeff would tell them, "She's not coming out." I was allowed to have company over, because my mom had met and approved of my friends. There were four of them now. For reasons I still don't understand, all my friends seemed to like my mother, so her apartment was the hangout spot. She was always generous, and if somebody was hungry, that person was welcome to eat anything we had in the house.

One afternoon, during the last fun, free days before summer ended and school began, we had a house full of my new friends. Everyone was sitting in the living/dining room area enjoying each other, laughing at the jokes my mom told them about me. I was cutting paper for a book I had written for my sisters that my baby sister was going to illustrate. For unknown reasons, anger boiled inside me, and I cut my four friends with the scissors—not deeply, not more than a scratch, but the laughter stopped.

My mind had been racing with thoughts of how phony this scene was. She isn't happy and pleasant with me! Why is she saying things about me to embarrass me? They're laughing at me.

I exploded with a rage born from taking too much and holding it all inside me.

"What the fuck is wrong with you? Are you crazy, Sheena? Go in your room!"

I couldn't move. The scene transfixed me. My mom ignored me. She had been a nurse when I was a child and was generally quick in her responses. She went to the medicine cabinet, brought back peroxide and Band-Aids, made a fuss over them.

Then she distributed oatmeal raisin cookies and juice and had them laughing again. I was rooted to that spot, with the scissors dangling from my left hand. *What did I do? Why did I do that?* Strangely, I felt empty at that point. The anger was gone. My friends were probably gone too, so I lied, "I was just playing. I didn't think they would cut. I'm sorry."

I was sorry, and children are resilient and forgiving. The moment had passed. After school, my new friend Rachel came to visit.

"Let's sit in the hallway."

"Okay, Rach, but why?"

"Mr. Jeff makes me uncomfortable."

"Yeah—tell me about it! Anyway, what's up?"

A few of the boys from school joined us in the hallway. We were laughing and talking innocently, but Jeff flipped.

"Sheena, get in this house! What are you doing sitting in these niggas' faces?"

"See y'all at school tomorrow. I'm on punishment for cutting my friends."

"Yup, Na is crazy," Rachel said, laughing. "Come on, boys."

The next day, Rachel and I were walking from school. "Na, everybody thinks Jeff is fucking you because of the way he acts."

I didn't respond. I didn't know how to. My book bag seemed to double in weight. I took it off my back and put my arm through the straps.

"You're my best friend and I know it's true. I can tell."

I knew when I heard her that I was right: Every girl was being molested.

"It happened to you too?" I whispered, although no one was near enough to hear us.

She looked away from me and said, "Let's change the subject. I think Calvin likes you."

I didn't want to change the subject. Rachel was a year older than me, and she was so calm and mature. I looked up to her. But she would say no more on the subject. Ever.

I listened to her talk about Calvin, his family, how often he checked me out. I didn't care. In school, after school, shopping, amusement parks, anywhere and everywhere we went, girls talked about boys and their dreams of boyfriends while I thought about finding a way to make this man stop pounding inside me and entertaining himself with my body.

❦

My cousin's birthday and mine are four days apart, and traditionally we celebrated together. I was turning twelve, and our gift from my mom was to get our hair done at a salon in styles of our choosing. We had our long hair relaxed for the first time and cut from the middle of our backs up to our shoulders.

That night when Jeff slithered into my bedroom, he was angry at the disappearance of my long ponytails. As a result, he was extremely rough with me. My secret place and surrounding areas would be sore for days.

Even with the light out, I could find a safe place inside the bare bulb that was screwed into a socket on the wall. But this night I couldn't completely black out. I couldn't find a crack in the ceiling; the room was too dark with the curtains closed.

Oh God, please let me die. Why do you keep letting him do this to me? Where is my mommy? It's my birthday. Why on my birthday? It's my day. God, help me.

My mind raced. Jeff pulled his penis out and I could feel hot slime shooting up my stomach.

Why won't the mattress open up and suck me inside it? Why can't I disappear this time?

I watched Jeff pull up his dingy gray sweatpants from around his knees as he walked toward the bathroom. I waited for the darkness to take me. It didn't. I waited for the mattress to suck in my numb, dirty, aching body. I wasn't good enough for that. He left a ball of tissue next to me. I wiped his gunk off my stomach, pulled my pajamas up, and listened to his retreating footsteps.

Is my mom home? Does she know what he's doing? Does she care?

These thoughts plagued me, and sleep eluded me. I wanted to curl up between my sisters for safety. How do they sleep through this? What would happen if I yelled and woke them up? Would he kill my sisters?

There was a door leading to the back balcony. I wrapped my blanket around me, put my slippers on, and unlocked the door. I breathed the freezing December air in and put my feet in the links of the fence. I was going to walk along the top rail until I fell off and crashed to the ground. I would probably land on one of the bags of garbage down there.

My slippers had elephants on them. The trunks were stuck in the fence links. After struggling to get them free, I lost the will or courage and went back inside. I snuggled between my sisters and fell asleep.

The next day, I took my sisters to school and then walked the few blocks to my junior high. Everything on my body ached, and I didn't want to deal with the whispering. The rumors about Jeff were circulating.

I strolled by my school and found a playground. There were no trees, but there were swings. I let the wind take me, but this playground wasn't secluded. A truant officer or cop could drive by at any time. So I took a long walk down Spring Garden Street to Seventh Street and walked up to the playground on Eighth in hopes of avoiding my mom if she was out. If she had spotted me, even from a block away, she would have roared my name, followed by a string of obscenities.

When school let out, I went home and made grilled cheese for me and my sisters. We followed that with fruit and two cookies. My middle sister was withdrawn, but she loved snacks. I hoped the cookies would bring her out of her mood. After coaxing her, she admitted that my baby sister started arguments with people but would then leave my middle sister to fight for her. It was natural for her to be protective; we were raised that way. But why was she sad and distant?

I sat them down to do their homework. Since I didn't have any, I sat down to watch cartoons. Jeff sidled up close to me and said, "Next time you get in bed with them, I'm getting in there too."

My stomach felt like he had just given it a punch.

"Do you do *that* to my sister?"

"No, but I will if you get in bed with them again."

I shut down again. I think he must have come back into the bedroom after I went to sleep. I began to wish I had walked along the top of the fence on the back balcony and jumped off.

On Valentine's Day, Mom gave each of us a box of Whitman's assorted chocolates and a teddy bear. She also bought me the Pierre Cardin jeans I had been asking for. On her birthday in April, we returned the favor with chocolates, a poem, and a soft, fluffy teddy bear.

I loved my teddy and would hold him tightly at night, hoping for protection. I'd look in his eyes and tell him all my secrets. I needed someone to confide in. I went to sleep holding him and my blanket tightly. Jeff woke me up by pulling my pajama bottoms and panties down. My eyes automatically searched for the bare bulb, but the light was off. I searched for my teddy, because Jeff only turned on the light when no one was home or if my mom was out. When she was out, he'd carry me to her bed.

For many months, the darkness refused to swallow me and the cracks would not rescue me. My body went rigid, my arms were plastered to my sides, and my legs were squeezed so tight I thought they'd cramp. Jeff easily pulled them apart and thrust his penis inside me. My teddy looked at me from the floor by my bed with accusatory eyes. I lay there as still as he was. I was as unable to protect myself as teddy was to protect me.

I didn't want to see the pain in teddy's eyes, so I closed mine and finally went numb. Without warning, Jeff jumped up and quickly attempted to pull up those familiar gray sweats while tripping toward the bathroom. The light came on.

Mom! My mom is here! I saw her and a part of me registered relief, but I couldn't fully come back to my body. My mouth wouldn't open.

Her eyes were wide, taking in the scene, and when she spoke, her words came out in rapid fire.

"Jeffrey, what the *fuck* are you doing?"

"Nothing."

I watched her eyes. She saw his bulge and the wet spot on his pants. For a minute, I was glad that it was on him and not on me this time. I hated it when his wetness got on me. I still do hate it whenever I remember.

She walked over, pulled back my blanket, and I saw her big eyes lower when she noticed that my pajamas weren't on. The whites of her eyes turned horror-movie red, and she shot past Jeff. Typical Jeff, he had to give me one last warning: "You better tell her it was the only time."

I stared into the light bulb and drifted while my mom's aluminum Louisville Slugger met with various parts of Jeff's body. My mom beat him out the door and away from me. My hero.

I was so relieved. *It's over now. She knows now. I love her. She protected me. Wait! Why is she screaming at me?*

"Is that why you wanted the pills? You wanted to fuck my man?"

What!

"Get the fuck outta my house, you fuckin' whore. Get out now!"

I could hear my sisters crying. I couldn't move. Why was she saying that? I didn't want him to do that to me.

"How long was this happening?"

You better tell her it was the only time.

"It was the only time." It would be over thirteen years before I told her the truth, but even then she couldn't stomach the details, so I omitted them.

"Get the fuck out *now*!"

My sisters' sobs were getting louder, but I couldn't look at them. I couldn't see the pain in their eyes or share the shame that I felt. I grabbed some clothes, dressed, and left in the middle of the night. My savior had sacrificed me.

I went to my friend Jessica's house on Eleventh Street. She told her dope-sick mother that my mom and I had argued and she'd put me out. Her mother allowed me to stay. I slept in Jessica's room. I woke up during the night with her older brother on top of me. I did what I had learned to do. I lay there and tried to escape my body, and the sour stench of his body.

When he finished with me, I rolled over and looked at my friend's bed, wondering if she was asleep or if she had quietly witnessed this violation. I wondered if he did that to her also.

I couldn't cry; I had run out of tears.

Nee Sims

My Shadow

I try to hide that I am fragile, that I hurt deep
And that most scars never heal.
I try to hide my pain at any cost.
What I want people to see when they see me is a woman
of strength and courage.
I want people to see me as a leader.
What truly makes me who I am is the pain I still struggle with.
I'm only as strong as my darkest secret.
I'm only as forgiving as my most tortured inner child.

I don't really think I want anyone to know me, because
I am such a complicated woman of sorts.
When I am in pain, I never shed a tear, well
occasionally one or two. On the inside,
I am yelling to be released. I weep and mourn
only in the depths of my soul.
I cringe at my ugly secrets.

I stare at the mirror and I know that the lady staring back at me
is not the same child who is deep within.

No one knows my pain.

I'm my own worst enemy. Ultimately my secrets will kill me.
The scars will never heal and the blood from my past
will thrust from within me just before I die.
There are so many tragedies in this one little body.

How the hell have I survived for so long?
The dark side that I try to hide is only reflected in my shadow.
I truly wish I could lie on the ground where my shadow is
and let my shadow lead my life. Without me,
my shadow does not exist, but even when I die,
my shadow is still there. The good thing about my shadow
is that no one can stare into her eyes
and know how empty she feels.

I'd like to swap places with my shadow.
It's so easy to lie there and just exist.

CHAPTER 7

July 1984

The next morning, my mother, sisters, aunt, and favorite cousin found me and took me home. My sisters knew my few friends and led my family to Jessica's house. The tension in our apartment was thick, and I didn't know what to do or say. My relationship with my mother altered drastically from that point. Something had ripped between us, and she didn't try to change it, or maybe she didn't know how.

My sisters also seemed distanced from me. I began to feel an unloved, lonely emptiness that I had not known before. We were never a loving, affectionate family, even before this. But after my mom found Jeff fleeing from my room, I felt as if I had been completely alienated.

On the streets, there were whispers and more gossip and speculation about my family. There was no relief anywhere. I needed my mother to talk to me. I was in turmoil every day.

"Sheena, what's the matter with you?" My mother's voice cut through the fog. Apparently, I had been sitting on the couch staring at the ceiling again.

"I don't know."

She rolled her eyes and continued walking to the kitchen. I was puzzled. How could I explain to her that there was so much that I didn't understand? That I loved Jeff like a dad and a friend. How could I love him when he did those things to me? Is that love? When you love somebody and they say they love you too, are you supposed to let them do what they want? If he loved me, why did he do to me what grown men do to women? Why don't I feel anything except crazy inside? Was it my fault because we used to play games? Did I do something to turn him on? Was it my nightie? My mom said I wanted him. Did I want him without realizing it? Is that possible at nine years old? Am I a whore, like my mom said? Why did I let him do it? Why didn't I tell anybody?

My emotions were conflicted, and I desperately needed someone to help me sort it all through. I needed somebody to talk to, to listen to me, and to care.

In the Bible, in the book of Genesis chapter 34, the story is told of the defilement of Dinah, Jacob's (Israel's) daughter. She had been raped by a prince in the land they had journeyed to. What makes the story special to me is the reaction of two of her brothers. They were enraged and avenged the violation of their sister.

That's what I wanted. I wanted to matter enough so someone would defend me. I needed somebody to feel and understand what I felt. I wanted someone to be hurt and angry, to show more than apathy. I didn't have that. If I had, perhaps it could have made a difference.

Instead, the course of my life had changed. Gone was my youthful innocence and exuberance. I withdrew further into the shell of myself and tried to forget. I escaped to school, yet school no longer held my interest as it once had. I didn't care about anything.

I began to cut classes and resumed creating small lines on my forearms that no one noticed since no one was paying attention. I learned that alcohol helped me forget what had happened and numbed the pain from the dissolution of my relationship with my mom. I wouldn't drink during the week, because I had to make sure my sisters ate and went to school. But on the weekends…

Every weekend, I drank myself into oblivion. The type of liquor was of no consequence, as long as it helped me to forget for a while. My mother couldn't understand what was happening to me, and there was so much that I wanted to tell her, because I needed to know if there was something wrong with me. Each time I would attempt to reach out to her, however, her words would reverberate in my mind: "You're a whore."

Even after years of therapy and healing, I still half-jokingly refer to myself as a whore, because I made her words my reality.

I stopped reaching to her for answers, for love, for acceptance. Instead, I opened my arms to boys.

One day I was watching *Oprah*, which was rare because I am a cartoon enthusiast. There was a segment on women who had suffered from childhood molestation and incest. Here was raw anger and tears, but I thought, *What's wrong with them? I'm twelve and I'm over it! They're like thirty and forty and still crying over* that*? It's done and over with! Get over it!*

I can recall the moment with clarity, because I was enraged. To me, their tears were a sign of an inability to let it go. I believed what I said. I believed it was done and over with. It happened and that was that. I believed that it didn't affect me, but of course I was wrong.

I was a study in contradictions. In the streets, guys noticed my curves, but their stares and lewd comments embarrassed me. I wanted the attention, but I was afraid of where it would lead. I was convinced that men wanted to degrade me. I didn't think I had anything else to offer. When I looked in the mirror, I didn't see an attractive young girl. I saw a dead thing with flat eyes that had forgotten how to laugh. I glimpsed a girl who didn't know her worth or potential.

I thought I had all the answers. (I couldn't get them from the one person who I had once believed had all the answers.)

I knew what needed to be done. Because I was shy, I didn't make the first move, but just about any boy who wanted it, got it. I feared men, so I would only date boys my age, no more than a year or two older. Date? Let's be honest, it wasn't dating; it was sex. The more I punished myself by permitting my body to be used for someone else's pleasure, the more I felt like I was paying somebody back. I was taking control of my life—I thought.

In essence, however, Jeff still had control of my life. I thought my choices were my own, but I was simply using what I had learned from him to bring ecstasy to others while being used by them. I wasn't taking back my life; I was continuing an abusive pattern. I hated what felt like a betrayal by my body, and I thought I could change this feeling if I convinced myself that I was now using that same body to fulfill my own will—but was I?

My first boyfriend was also twelve, and we allowed our friends to persuade us to have sex. We lay on an itchy wool blanket at the playground near the swimming pool. I glanced repeatedly at my Q-bert game watch while he flopped around inside and outside of me because I had not learned to tighten a vagina that had been stretched by an adult. This was just the beginning of many sexual encounters—with men and women—that failed to satisfy my body but fulfilled my self-loathing. Anger became my motivating factor and driving force.

I didn't hate men in general; I hated the feeling of helplessness. I hated the child in me that had no control over my own body or the man who had invaded my secret place. Sex was my weapon and my coping mechanism, while alcohol was my balm. I didn't entice, because I didn't view myself as sexy, but I used what I had learned: how to make myself believe that I was taking charge of the situation and had total control over what did and didn't happen to me. It was a baffling time, because my body was busy trying to move forward in the only way I knew how, but my heart was in turmoil.

I still loved Jeff, and I deeply loved my father and missed seeing him. I was their firstborn, and when my parents were together I spent every available moment with my father. When he was a student at Temple University, his electives were photography and martial arts. I was at his matches and a favorite model for his tripod. He loved basketball, so I was his cheerleader when he played, or else we cheered side by side at Sixers games.

I missed my father. I loved my daddy. There was no end to my confusion. He never raised his voice at me. He never hit me. Still, he hurt me and I loved him. Wasn't it normal to love your family despite anything? Was I wrong for loving my father but hating my mother? Was I normal? What was normal, and how could I get back to it? Should I forget that all of this happened so I can go back to loving my mother and sitting in the stadium with my father? How do I go back? Repeatedly, I asked myself another question: *Will my dad try it again?*

I didn't know about normal, because it had never been clearly defined for me. And I didn't know what the boundaries of love were either. I knew I wanted to be my father's daughter, and that's why I continued to try. As a child, I made excuses for his behavior and rationalized his actions—he was drunk and on drugs—much the way women do when their husbands hit them. Nevertheless, in actuality, rape is akin to murder, because they both extinguish the light that's in you, and your family has to mourn who you once were while desperately trying to put the pieces back together and move forward. Sadly, once there's been a violation, you are forever changed and you carry its indelible mark. You may become prey for the predators.

Once I realized this, I wanted to change it. I began to write. When an interview and various poems were published, however, my family refused to read my work. None of them understood that writing was a part of my healing. In their view, the child I had been was dead, buried, and didn't require a resurrection. They couldn't quite grasp that it was essential for me to share my experiences so other survivors of sexual abuse and dysfunctional families would know they weren't alone. I had to rid myself of the shame, because it was crippling. My body had healed physically, but psychologically I was shattered, and the experience needed to be shared. There was no way to remove the stench of shame and revulsion for me, because I felt that it was my fault.

The shame is what led to my destructive behaviors—led to the cutting, the hair pulling, the head banging, and other acts of self-mutilation including alcoholism, promiscuity, and violence inflicted on others. I've often reflected on why, while the majority of victims take the route I did, there are also many, like Oprah, Donnie McClurkin, and Tyler Perry, who don't. I wonder if the outlet someone has chosen and their upbringing make a difference. For instance, Donnie, my favorite gospel singer, chose the church and choir. Some had therapy, while still others found solace in school.

I needed to destroy myself, however, and none of those places offered that option.

Still, their lives inspired me. So I started writing and continue to write in an attempt to understand myself and my life, to help someone else on his or her journey.

After the molestation ended and prior to therapy, I was raped three times, and on one other occasion there was an attempted rape. After therapy, not once. Before I sought therapy, I sought out victimization.

Never one to be alone, my mother soon found a new boyfriend, Daymond. He moved in with us and quickly won over my sisters. But I was hesitant. In time, he wore down my defenses and I began to like him. After considerable time, I loved him. His family visited frequently, and they treated us as children, not objects of desire. My mother is quick to boast that all of her daughters are very pretty. And after Jeff, her eyes had become watchful. She noticed that Daymond showed no signs of lust for her children. He never has, and I'm certain he never will.

One day, not long after my fourteenth birthday, I was home alone, struggling with feelings of loneliness and depression. I felt ugly, unloved, and unwanted. My fingertips were burning, because I had bitten my fingernails down to the quick, and my hands looked mannish and malformed—especially since I had developed the habit of hitting walls and cracking my knuckles, much to my aunt's disapproval.

Then Draymond's cousin showed up at the door. When I let him in, he went to the kitchen to make something to eat. I readjusted my shirt to expose my shoulder and bra strap. I stretched out seductively on the couch and pretended to fall asleep. After he had eaten and returned to the living room, he carefully fixed my shirt and sat down to watch television and wait for Daymond.

It seemed as if I remained in that position for hours, amazed that he didn't take advantage of me. I couldn't dig myself out of confusion, because I constantly created new situations that added to my befuddlement. I was disappointed that he didn't want me, but I questioned my actions and subsequent feelings of relief. He didn't actually appeal to me, and sex was not gratifying for me. It was simply my answer for anything, particularly if I was bored, depressed, or feeling unattractive. It was a void filler, giving me what I didn't have: power.

However, I gave that power away continually.

❦

I was in an endless cycle of wanting control yet giving it away when I sat on the toilet a few months before my fourteenth birthday and learned I still had no control over my own body. I was in excruciating pain, sweating, and pushing distractedly. I was in a panic, afraid that my mom would see the trail of blood from my bed to the bathroom. I had never seen so much blood.

"Wake up. Something's wrong with me. My stomach hurts so bad!" I cried to my youngest sister.

"You want me to wake Mommy up?"

"No, I'm going to the bathroom." My stomach cramped as if I had to defecate. I stood up and the room started spinning. Blood literally poured down my legs and I felt faint. I looked down between my legs and saw what I hoped was a blood clot. My cycles were heavy from the onset, so I was no stranger to clots. But this was different; it didn't just drop into the toilet. I touched it.

"Sis!" She had been putting newspaper on my bloody path. God bless her. My mom wouldn't see it. She looked at me with huge eyes. Her pouty mouth formed a small circle, a question left unasked.

I tugged it gently and saw five toes.

"Oh God!" I could feel the color drain from my face. My sister steadied me; the floor was rushing up to meet me.

"I'm getting Mommy."

I couldn't talk. I didn't talk in the ambulance to the hospital. I couldn't talk when my baby, my boy, was unceremoniously stuffed in a specimen container. This should have changed me. It did, but not in the way that it could have. Instead, I learned how easy it is to deny more than just sexual violations. I could also deny a miscarried baby whose father lived with another woman and had a child with her. I could deny that I had been wrestling with my sisters while knowing that Mom-Mom dreamed about fish (somebody's pregnant) and my dad's sister felt certain I was pregnant ("Look at how light your hands are!"). I could deny anything except my future visits to hospital emergency rooms and the children I would give birth to (a daughter two weeks after my sixteenth birthday and a son at eighteen).

Later, between the birth of my daughter and my son, I would miscarry twin boys. At that point, something inside me snapped.

"You would have loved your big sister. She's the best thing that ever happened to me."

I lovingly caressed the first fetus, this boy, my boy, and briefly wondered why the bluish cord was still inside me.

"Where's the afterbirth?"

He felt not quite right, but that didn't matter as I held him in the palm of my hand and looked at his toes, his fists, his closed eyelids with lashes. "You were going to look like your dad, I can tell."

After some time passed, my mother left to get ready for work and I again watched a fetus find its way into a specimen container.

"Ms. King."

I turned to glare at the doctor who lacked respect for my baby.

"What!"

"We are going to have to surgically remove the placenta."

"Why?"

"Because it has not come out on its own."

The doctor informed me that I could die if it remained inside me. I didn't care. The afterbirth had not come out on its own because there was another baby inside me.

With white sheets pulled up to my chin, I stared at the wall until the father of my fetuses came to pick me up. We rode in silence from Broad Street to Tenth and Brown. He held my hand in his, but I could not feel it.

"Mom, you have to believe me. I saw my other baby and they are lying, he was alive!"

"Girl, are you crazy? So what did they do to your baby?"

"I don't know, but I know what I saw."

"You were under anesthesia."

"I wasn't under yet. I felt him come out and I saw him—he was alive!"

"Where's the death certificate?"

"What?"

"The death certificate," my mother said, enunciating those three words as if I was mentally challenged.

"I don't have one. Nobody gave me one."

"And you don't have twins that are alive either."

I went to bed that night with my daughter beside me. I told her about her brothers and promised her that I would give her a real live brother when the time was right. I kept that promise, but I have never forgotten the three sons that my wild and fast life took from me.

Denial proves beneficial for a short time, but reality won't remain hidden. I tried to deny my follow-up Pap smear because I didn't want to obsess about it. I had planned to forget it. I didn't want to know the results. If I could deny they were ever there, then they wouldn't be, right?

I had tried that before, after the birth of my daughter. My Pap smear was abnormal, and a colposcopy was done—a biopsy of the small area of malformed cervical cells.

"On a scale of one to five, with one being normal and five being cancer, you are a three," my ob-gyn informed me with her right hand raised to give me a visual aid—as if I needed one.

Denial worked for almost two decades, or perhaps it was the colposcopy. When you live your life denying what's real, the line between truth and fantasy becomes distorted in every area. In a relationship, your eye may be black, your front teeth knocked out, but you tell yourself and others, "He loves me and he gets real angry when other guys look at me." You've stepped over that blurred line from reality to fantasy. Many people who have suffered from childhood trauma will find themselves living on the borderline, precariously between neurotic and psychotic. I've walked that balance beam.

Nee Sims

Love Is Not

You don't know any better. What are these feelings you've got?
You have a hunger brewing but let me tell you what love is not.
It won't take you for granted or laugh when your heart knocks.
Won't judge you by your looks cuz that's what love is not.
You spread your legs and let it in, you think that's what love means.
But hear me little angel: love is not between your knees.
You offer up your treasure hoping someone will treat it well.
But love won't disregard you or find satisfaction in your outer shell.
It's not something easy that comes along every day.
It's nurturing and understanding, won't impatiently walk away.
You think you know what love is so you pour it in a golden pot.
Some thief walks by and gets excited; a fool that knows
what love is not!
Abandon trust, an eye for lust, someone please take what I have:
a twinkle in your hungry eyes, they know this is what love is not.
Open your legs and let them in while your heart is tied in knots.
Sex and smile, let's play awhile ... this is what love is not!

CHAPTER 8

March 1985

I have never been addicted to drugs, and, frankly, it took many, many years of listening to "war stories" before I was able to understand the concept or relate it to anything I had experienced. I didn't know want, hunger, or desperation. What I craved wasn't tangible. It was love. So I couldn't comprehend the lengths people were driven to for drugs.

I watched and wondered. I drank forties—forty-ounce bottles of beer—with the guys. I boldly purchased Wild Irish Rose, Mad Dog 20/20, Malt Duck, and other beverages from any speakeasy that would serve me. Honestly, I never found one that wouldn't serve me, or any other minor.

Times were hard. Morals were low. I drank myself pissy every weekend from age twelve until I was eighteen, except during my pregnancies. I couldn't see anything wrong in drinking on weekends, because I went to school, took care of my sisters, and didn't drink during the week. I learned this from my Mom-Mom. She was a schoolteacher who worked every day until she retired, went to church every Sunday, but was drunk every Friday and Saturday until "Jesus saved her from sin." I didn't steal, didn't sell my possessions or myself for alcohol, so I couldn't be an alcoholic. Right?

Years later, I acknowledged that I used alcohol to banish my demons, lessen my pain, and override my shyness. I was still an alcoholic, but I fooled myself into believing that I was somehow superior to drug addicts. I saw firsthand how drugs destroyed families and ruined lives. I shook my head when I saw girls with whom I went to school losing drastic amounts of weight, wearing greasy scarves and dirty baseball caps over uncombed, unwashed, matted hair. The guys on the corners would share stories about having grown women give several of them blow jobs, one after another, for a five-dollar vial of crack. This amazed and angered me simultaneously. How could women in their mid-thirties give young teenage boys blow jobs for drugs? I didn't understand.

It wasn't everyone's story, but it was the dominant reality I could see. There were a few who would take their teenage daughters with them to get their welfare checks. They'd give the money and food stamps to their responsible children so rent could be paid and food and clothes purchased. Then they would smoke what was left. They called themselves "functional addicts." In my immaturity, they seemed far superior to the pregnant women who smoked crack and the ones who sold their children or allowed men to have sex with them for drugs.

I sat on the front step of my apartment building or the corner of my block with my forty-ounce and watched all of this, periodically dodging bullets from drive-by shootings.

Years later, in group sessions for AOD (alcohol and other drugs), I would remember my drunken stupors and the realities of addiction. Now, just as I did then, I watch and I listen. Commodities aren't the same where I presently reside, but the desperation, the want, the hunger are identical.

Two rolled cigarettes (from a pack of tobacco that nets thirty to forty rolled cigarettes and costs $2.46 a pack) will get you ten to twenty dollars of commissary items. Psychotropic, high-blood-pressure, or nerve pills are sold from two to five dollars each, and if someone happens upon any medication whose effects are similar to heroin, she can make an easy sixty to a hundred dollars.

Sex can also be traded for cigarettes and pills. Addiction doesn't end simply because of incarceration. It continues to flourish, and when those who thrive on it are released to the streets, most return to prison if they haven't overdosed. I shake my head and think back with regret on the life I chose in the spring of 1985.

I didn't recognize the dangers of the streets because I had adapted to them. The things that I had feared when I moved from Mount Airy to the projects were now commonplace. Violence was an everyday occurrence, and I had learned the code of the streets: You see everything but see nothing, as you actively forget what you've seen. Keep your head down, shoulders hunched so no one remembers you and you remember no one. I had learned every code: Trust no one, demand respect, and if you don't get it, you take it.

Most of my knowledge of the streets came from Robbie. I met him on a rainy Saturday afternoon.

I had a taste for chicken. I threw on a pair of blue Jordache jeans, a red button-down shirt under a blue-and-red argyle sweater with matching socks, blue Nike Air Maxes, dark-blue Nike windbreaker, and a red-and-blue baseball cap with an *A* on the front.

"Na, where you goin'?" my youngest sister asked.

"Broad Street."

Today I wanted to be alone. I was feeling especially depressed, and I preferred solitude when I was in a black mood. I didn't want to take it out on my sisters.

I walked from Tenth Street to Broad, hoping the steady rain would clear my head and wash away my suicidal thoughts. My mind was racing and I couldn't focus on any one particular thing, so I allowed it to roam as I strolled, with my head down, trying to avoid puddles in a city of potholes—nearly impossible!

I decided to sit on the first-floor landing of our four-story apartment building so the family I was feeling hatred for that day wouldn't disturb me. I didn't care that I was wet and the brim of my cap was dripping rain on my bucket of chicken and biscuits. I didn't care about anything. I watched the rainfall through the open door until a man filled the doorway.

He wore all red: sweatpants, sweatshirt, and white-and-red shell tops. He had a round face and big round eyes.

"Is Lorna home?" he asked.

I jerked my greasy thumb to the left to indicate which apartment she lived in. There were two apartments on each floor. He knocked on her door, and I took another bite of a crispy chicken breast before informing him, "She's not home. She went to see her mom."

In a small apartment building, everyone knows everyone's business. Some months later, when Daymond began smoking crack and property started to disappear from our apartment, everyone knew before the boys that worked for me (more about that shortly) told me. People knew before the weight loss and the unexplained withdrawals from our savings account. Everyone knew everyone else's business.

With my eyes shielded by the brim of my cap, I watched Robbie with curiosity. *Where did he come from? I've never seen him around here before. Is he Lorna's boyfriend?* Lorna was eighteen and had the apartment to herself after her mom moved and she took over the rent. I had been there a number of times drinking, and Lorna hadn't mentioned a boyfriend.

"Are you Larry's father?" I asked when curiosity got the best of me. I was surprised at myself, because I didn't talk to men I didn't know. Hell, I didn't talk to *anyone* I didn't know and spoke very little to the people I did know.

"Larry? Oh, Lorna's son. No, I'm not his father. Lorna and I went to school together." He smiled and his eyes crinkled at the corners. He told me about their time in high school. I was in junior high, so I was a little impressed. High school sounded cool. Unfortunately, once I went to high school, I had only one friend and we were both painfully shy. I was usually hung over and cutting classes to sneak home and sleep it off, or in some boy's bed. So my experience was markedly different from the picture he painted.

Robbie told me that he had grown up in the projects but was incarcerated for a few years. "Oh, that's why I never saw you before," I said. I had heard stories about juvenile facilities from my play brother Andre and my Uncle Kev, but I hadn't been there. I had come close when a friend convinced me that we could prop the door open at school and run to the store for chips and Snickers at lunchtime. Like most things, however, we hadn't thought this through, and we found ourselves locked out. Our school was close enough to walk to Center City, so we went to the Gallery, a mall. My "friend" thought it would be fun to pull the fire alarm—until the security guards caught us. My mom believed me when I told her that I didn't do it.

"You're a stupid-ass follower with no mind of your own!" she shouted as she hit me with a switch on our walk home from the basement security center of the Gallery. I might as well have pulled the alarm, since I had to put up with her screaming at me and calling me names anyway.

I received probation because I was an honor roll student, but probation wasn't enough for me. I was arrested two years later for carrying an unconcealed weapon after a fight with a boy, who had once been my friend, because he shouted that I was a whore and a slut. My mother took me to the Youth Study Center, where I was given a date for family court. She didn't take me to court, however. My Mom-Mom did.

"I'm sick of you! Go to court by yourself. I have two other children to worry about, and I'm tired of your dumb ass! I should have given you to my mother when she asked me!"

"What? Nana's mean and she don't even like you," I smarted back.

"When you were five, she said to give you to her because you were just like her and she could tell that you were going to go to jail just like she did."

Those words proved to be prophetic. If I had known, I would not have listened to Robbie. I would have continued to listen to the rain hit the tin roof over the door.

Robbie talked about his brothers and his mother, and I could hear the love and protectiveness that he felt for his family. They seemed like a close-knit family. Secretly, so deep inside myself that I was in defiance of it, I wanted the same thing. He spoke of respect and loyalty among friends and family, but to me, those things only existed on television shows like *The Cosby Show*, *The Brady Bunch*, *Diff'rent Strokes*, and *Family Ties*. I would watch those shows and hate my life because it wasn't and could never come close to those lived by the TV characters. I would try to turn from them to cartoons or comedies, because I could laugh and not ache with longing for a life that appeared to me to be more of a fantasy than a talking rabbit or flying mouse was.

Although Robbie had me captivated, I was still slightly surprised by my response, after listening to him talk for an hour, when he said, "Little girl, what do you want to be when you grow up?"

"A drug dealer."

His mouth opened in surprise and his eyes sparkled, but he didn't miss a beat. I will never forget this moment, because it was the end of my life. I didn't hesitate to formulate my answer; there it was. Before his question, I hadn't considered it. I had observed the camaraderie among the young boys on the corners. I had watched how they appeared to have each other's backs and made sure everybody ate. I had heard them calling out, "Five-O" to protect everyone from being arrested. I watched and pondered but hadn't considered it.

I listened to Robbie. "So, if I gave you an ounce, what would you do with it?"

"Sell it," was my sarcastic response, because he should have known that answer.

"How?"

"Umm … well—I don't know."

He laughed, but he knew how, and he taught me. I had heard stories of my father selling drugs, my grandfather getting over by hustling real estate, and his father making a fortune from moonshine in North Carolina. I convinced myself that hustling was "in my blood."

As I had been taught to put all I had into sex, I was instructed to do the same with the hustle. I had already learned to avoid emotional attachments. Years of abuse created a bitter, angry blackness inside me. I would be nicknamed Ice Princess, Boss Lady, and Gangsta Bitch by the guys who worked with and for me, or who hung on the corners.

Melanie Vicheck

The Pounding of the Shower

the pounding of the shower
pretending to wash away the pain
to empty my mind
and not go insane

tell me nothing happened
it couldn't have been rape
you weren't just inside of me
and these bruises are fake

the ones on my shoulders
are not from the wall
you didn't slam me against it
not once, not at all

the ones on my thighs
couldn't have come from you
you didn't force yourself inside of me
I imagined that too

the one on my ass
wasn't from the floor
I didn't fall to the ground
after you snuck out the door

that wasn't me
crawling across the floor
those weren't my tears
that everyone ignored

I wasn't the one
who knew she couldn't tell

but I'm starting to wonder
if I was the one who fell

those thoughts weren't mine
I never want to look
back to that horrible morning
to the day you took my soul

I wasn't the one
whose life was changed
I wasn't the one
who felt the shame

sleep with one,
sleep with them all
that was his reason
so maybe I did take a fall

I guess time will tell
if I can heal
when I can admit
that the event was real

CHAPTER 9

January 1987

He stepped out of a dark-blue Mercedes in textured caramel-colored leather pants and jacket. I slowly took him in while his back was turned, revealing muscular shoulders and firm buttocks. I paid for my bag of Herr's potato chips and Elliott's apple juice and put the change in the front pocket of my jeans.

"Hey, come here."

"Hay is for horses."

"Come here, girl."

I walked slowly, trying to figure out a way to gain control of the situation.

"Turn around."

"What?"

"*Can* you turn around?"

I did, face flushed, knowing this man was staring at my ass. His tone didn't elicit fear, but it invited my trademark sarcasm. "See anything you like?"

"I do, get in." Something about his manner caused me to obey. Perhaps I was accustomed to or trained to follow orders from older commanding men, or maybe I was looking for something else to take me out of my misery. I don't know what it was, but the confidence of this man intrigued me.

What I do know is that we talked for fifteen minutes and he invited me to dinner. We ate at Penn's Landing on a beautiful ship, and I felt out of my element—as if people were staring at me and judging us, thinking we didn't belong. But Kevin possessed an air of authority that was comforting.

He introduced me to fine dining, shopping with no thought of cost, and the intricacies of the world of D-boy ("dope boy," or drug dealer) bosses. The glitz and glamour of that world was fantastic in a material sense, but it was also a life of paranoia, secrecy, distrust, and danger.

My mother viewed him as arrogant and disrespectful, but I eventually saw a side of him that had been hurt and was deeply insecure. Girls are programmed with a desire to save hurting boys.

In the beginning, there were often tests of trust. He'd leave money lying around. He'd send me places with people who worked for him. There were so many tests—and by passing all of them, I was able to gain Kevin's trust. Our relationship changed also. We went from less expensive champagne to Dom, from motels to hotels with gourmet chocolate on the pillow to his apartments in gated communities, from the latest sneakers to expensive shoes, jewelry, and clothes that had tags engraved with names I could barely pronounce.

We also graduated to experimentation and abuse. I thought those days were gone and forgotten, but the cycle of abuse always continued, it simply wasn't as obvious to me. There was a shop in Chinatown that we'd frequent where Kevin bought pills that were supposed to heighten the sexual experience. Even with a chilled bottle of Dom, those horse pills would lodge in my throat! There didn't seem to be any difference in his performance or our encounters, but he thought they had a major impact.

I hooked up with Kevin often for about a year, but often wasn't enough. The emptiness in me still needed to be filled with the only things I knew that could satisfy me: alcohol, danger, and more sex. When Kevin returned from one of his many trips, he picked me up and drove us to the Hilton.

"Get on your knees!"

I smiled, thinking he was joking. He slapped me hard across my face. This wasn't the first time he had done that. The first time we were in his Pathfinder going to dinner. I assumed we were going to Walnut Street, but when he came to a halt at a stop sign in Chinatown, he asked me, "Do you want Chinese?"

"I don't really like Chinese food."

"I'm not talking about Chinese storefronts in the projects!"

"Kevin, I didn't come from the projects, we moved there because we had a fire. My family and I go to restaurants often, and I don't really like Chinese food. It's alright, but I don't want—"

Before I finished my sentence, his hand went back and forth across my face in rapid succession, while he yelled, "Don't tell me no!"

I didn't say anything at all while I slowly ate pepper steak with rice at Ho Sai Gai.

I thought of this former incident as I tried to read his face this time for signs of humor. He slapped me again.

"Get on your fuckin' knees!"

Defiantly, I stood there with my hand to my cheek, wondering where this was coming from. He gave me several rib shots, and I fell to my knees in front of him. He roughly grabbed my already burning face and squeezed my cheeks to open my mouth. As if I had been transported backward through time, this was me at nine years old being forced to do what I didn't want to do. Inside, I was screaming at myself, *Bite it off, bite it off,* but I couldn't move.

He held the back of my head and quickly pumped his hips. From a great distance, it seemed, I could hear him screaming obscenities and asking me, "You like fucking my boys? You like fucking them. I saw the pictures!" *What pictures? What is he talking about?*

The more he screamed and pumped, the further I retreated inside myself. I hate being yelled at. I automatically shut down. I felt him dragging me across the floor to the end of the bed, where he sat down, never releasing the grip on the back of my head.

I assumed he was tired, because he put both hands on the sides of my face and moved my head back and forth. When he began to ejaculate, I vomited on him, on the bed, and on the floor. I suppose it was the gag reflex and part of me was satisfied at his anger and revulsion, but that satisfaction was short lived. He didn't punch me in my face, but my body was punished before he dropped me off at my door.

I sat soaking in the tub, telling myself that I'd never let a man hit me again. I don't know if Kevin saw a change in me or if I had just learned enough about him to avoid upsetting him, but he didn't hit me again. Maybe he knew a truth that I hadn't accepted yet, although I felt it.

"Are you pregnant?" he asked me one night.

"What?"

We were spooning, with his hand caressing my flat stomach. "No, I'm not pregnant."

Softly he said, "I think you are."

I was. Kevin and I slowly drifted apart.

I had dreams of making a better life for the baby growing in my belly, so I hustled harder, thinking that was the way to provide it. I sold drugs and moved guns. I hadn't made the conscious choice to stop drinking, snorting coke occasionally, and smoking Newports. The baby inside me made that choice for me. Whenever I tried to drink or smoke a cigarette, I became ill. I guess that my baby girl didn't want any of that stuff in her body, so I lost the craving for all of it.

I tried to change, I wanted to, and when the streets became dangerous, I went looking for a job. Nevertheless, I had convinced myself that the streets were the only thing I knew, that I had no other talents except sex and hustling.

Sheena King

Unforgiving Desert

The sun, its unforgiving blaze, no shade,
no spray for malevolent bugs—they bite,
they sting,
        they dig through skin,
burrow in deep.

I lose my way as I travel without
guidance through this barren land. My
feet retract as they tread weather-worn patches of earth.
Their flesh, cut, leaves a mottled trail as I stumble forward.

But now a stretch of sand expands
as far as the eye can see,
further than the mind can comprehend.
A searing wind whips around me, spinning
grains individually,
collectively,
 furiously,
blindingly.

My feet sink. The weight of the world
presses me into these dunes. I open my mouth
to scream; dust fills my parched throat.
I succumb, acquiesce to the pull until
a hand stretches toward me, drags me
back into the open air, holds me tightly.

The heat subsides, the
pain dissipates—
My Oasis?
No.
It is only you:
My Mirage.

Journal Entry: April 2, 1998

I have come to a place in my life where I begin to notice a pattern of numerous relationships of quick starts and even quicker finishes. I questioned why I was fortunate to have several good people but I couldn't sustain the relationship. I didn't know then that relationships are work required by two people. I believed it was my fault alone. Yet, even in hindsight, I have to admit that the majority of the problems in my relationships were my own creation. I lay in bed that night, awake until after 4:00 a.m. going backward through my life. I wasn't looking for anyone to blame. I wasn't looking for instability patterns or more signs and symptoms of the borderline personality or emotionally unstable personality disorder that I was diagnosed with. I wasn't having a pity party of abuse. I was trying to understand myself. It was crucial that I learn why I did the things that I was doing. Why did I sabotage my relationships? Why did I find great satisfaction and relief in hurting the ones who loved me? Why did I cry in anguish after I ruined a relationship, even when I knew I wasn't in love? What was my problem? I watched the scenes of my life play backward then forward and back again. I fought to deny what my memories were showing me. What I carefully suppressed was the key to why and how I had become who and how I was: my childhood abuses. I didn't want to accept it as true, because it felt like a cop-out, as if I was making excuses for my behavior. This didn't sit well with me, because I believed in taking responsibility for my own actions and not trying to find ways to excuse them. I tried for a number of hours to compel my mind and heart to accept another reason—maybe I was just evil. My mom said I was the spawn of Satan because I didn't like church and would become physically ill if she made me attend. Maybe she was right or maybe I just haven't learned how to have a relationship.

Prison taught me that friendships must balance and not take from me while I gave without hesitation. Maybe I needed lessons. Maybe they were wrong for me. I struggled against the obvious, because it seemed lazy—just give it all to the obvious. It seemed too textbook, too talk-showish, but it was true. I really couldn't deny it, because one thing about truth is, once it's been revealed, it refuses to be denied or to return to the dark places where we cast it. It was true. I had arrived at that fork in my road where I could continue as I was, happy in my misery, finding satisfaction and relief from my pain by hurting other people, or I could be uncomfortable. Before I eventually drifted to sleep in those early morning hours, I realized that I didn't take pleasure in feeling abandoned when a relationship ended; however, I also didn't enjoy feeling love for someone else, because it came with too much, it cost too much, and I wasted too much time obsessing over him or her. I also realized that I wasn't loving anyone, I was trying to love myself through them, but I didn't find myself worthy of their love and I hadn't learned how to love. I wanted to end this tiresome cycle I'd created. There was no benefit to it, or real purpose for it.

As the sun rose, I rolled over on my stomach, intending to sleep for a few hours. I looked toward the window before I dozed, and for the first time in my life, I said, "Jesus, if you are real, help me. I don't want to be like this anymore." Before this pivotal night, I was comfortable with myself and unaware that anything was wrong with the way I was, but now I finally saw myself clearly. I also saw the horrible things I had done. "God, please forgive me." I had no more words. I didn't know if God could or would or if He existed. It was an act without consciousness. I began to cry, because I remembered begging God that my eye would stop hurting. He/She/It didn't answer me then. The buckle from my mom's belt sliced across my left eye and my favorite cousin in her seven-year-old wisdom told me to lie down in the recess yard and stare at the sun so my eye would feel better. Of course it didn't, just as the hot bath didn't soothe my back after my mom stomped me with her sneakers on when I was five years old for writing the number two backward.

Before drifting off to sleep, I thought, I have to get some help. I have to get right for me and my children.

CHAPTER 10

October 1988

The breakup with Kevin was just another phase of men entering and exiting my life. It was unspoken. He simply stopped coming around, and I stopped looking for him. I was understandably surprised when, shopping with my mother one day, I ran into him.

It was an unseasonably nice autumn day. I was seven months pregnant, huge with my first child. My feet were aching, and I stared down at them as if the concentrated glaring would make a difference, as if it would magically ease the pain. When I looked up, Kevin was walking toward us with his eyes on my bulging belly. He walked right past us and softly spoke five words: "I knew you were pregnant."

I have never seen Kevin again. Several years later, while I was in the Philadelphia county jail, Kevin's cousin, Ice, told me that he'd had a seizure while driving and had died. I didn't want to believe it. Had it been anyone other than his cousin, I wouldn't have believed it. She loved him and wouldn't have lied to me about that. When Kevin heard our daughter was born, he sent his sister and Ice to my apartment to see her. That was the norm for D-boys who had accumulated wealth and who had multiple sex partners—especially if the girl who claimed he was the father was not his main girl.

I was not his main girl, and although I was slightly offended, I did understand the game. I was well aware of how girls would "put babies" on a guy with money so the child would be taken care of—whether he was the real father or not. I knew girls who pretended to be pregnant only to collect abortion money from numerous guys. I wasn't that girl. Keven never pretended that he wanted more children than he already had. I knew he didn't. I also knew that I didn't need him to provide for my child. Nor did I need fake abortion money when I had every intention of keeping my daughter. I didn't think at all about the type of father he would be. I knew that he was dangerous and perhaps emotionally unstable, but those were the traits that linked us together. He had a death wish and I didn't care about living.

Instinctively, I knew that I needed Keeva, because she wanted to live. So I watched Ice and Kevin's sister, Angie, inspect my daughter without any concern about their thoughts. I had no reaction to Ice's words to her cousin when she said, "She's Kevin's. She looks just like you, Angie." None of that mattered, because Keeva was mine and at age sixteen I truly believed that all she and I needed was each other. She would be my reason to live.

It's probably better that Keeva and Kevin didn't know each other, because JBM, a powerful drug gang in Philadelphia, was taking over and demanded that all D-boys, especially those with considerable wealth, either "get down or lay down." Kevin had already told me some time before that he refused to "get down." So he lived in a state of paranoia. My daughter would have been just as affected by that as I was. It was a frightening time for everyone—not just people in the game but their families too, because bullets rained down on everyone. No one was really safe.

If there was any place that was semi-safe, however, it was my high school.

Keeva was born on December 19, fifteen days after my sixteenth birthday. The holiday break followed, and I then transferred to William Penn High, because it was closer to home than my old school, Edward Bok, which was in South Philly. Inside William Penn it was safe, but outside I was robbed at knifepoint on my way to school. On another occasion, my earrings were snatched by two teenage boys just outside of school. This didn't frighten or anger me greatly, because jewelry could be replaced.

What did anger me were the scratches I discovered one day on my baby's face.

My friend Lorna would watch Keeva while I was in school, because my mother worked. My two younger sisters were in school, and Keeva would have to be one year old before I could bring her to the school's day care. I was already apprehensive about leaving my child with anyone, as most first-time mothers are. Because of the abuse I had suffered, I was extremely protective of my daughter. So I would check Keeva thoroughly whenever she was in the care of someone else. I noticed the scratches on her face, so I removed her clothes, checked her Pamper to be sure she was dry and that her genitals were not disturbed. I asked Lorna about the scratches, and she said, "Maybe she did it herself."

I knew I kept her fingernails clipped, but I checked them anyway. No nails, no jagged edges—nothing.

"What the fuck did you do to my baby?"

By now I was in her face, all reason and rationality gone. She said, "Lawrence was playing with her."

Lawrence was a one-year-old adorable boy who was always into something. I couldn't blame him. But my daughter was two months old, and somebody needed to pay for the scratches on her face. In the end, I was the one who paid, because I refused to leave her with anyone.

I dropped out of school and later took my GED at a community college. I passed it on the first try, then took an application to enroll in the college. I wanted to major in psychology, because I had an overwhelming interest in the human mind and its behaviors. I desperately wanted to run a shelter for women and children so their experiences could be better than mine.

When I told my mother, she said, "I could see you billing me a hundred dollars an hour, but for a shelter it's going to cost lots of money to operate and employ people to run it and maintain it." She brought me crashing right back to earth. As she droned on and on, the only words I heard were, "It's going to take money, and lots of it."

Robbie was my friend, but more importantly, I was his friend, his confidante. I believed in me because he believed in me.

"Sheena, do you think I'm crazy?"

"Huh? Why would you say that? No."

I sat up on the bed and stared at him, because his voice sounded strange. He was sitting on the end of my bed and resting his chin on his hand, looking broken. His words were laced with a sadness I had only heard when he spoke about his family, especially his father.

"Because of what I do."

"You're a businessman."

"I'm a hit man."

"That's not what you are, it's sometimes what you do, Robbie. You have to do what's necessary, right? That's what you taught me."

I downed my forty-ounce of Coqui 900 and lit a Newport, preparing for more of this unusual conversation, but Robbie grew quiet. I tried to push the question from my mind; it would be disloyal to think of my friend the way he was describing himself. Although the JBM was a powerful force, our business prospered under Robbie's supervision. Still, my hold on reality diminished as I sank further into the fantasy I had created. Unaware, I had convinced myself that I wasn't causing harm to anyone. I was operating a business and taking care of my family. I had become comfortable with and thrived in my role as protector and provider. I reasoned that no one had protected me or provided emotional stability, so I would protect and provide in the only way that I knew how.

Yet, deep inside me, on a subconscious level, I craved a protector and provider. I wanted to be able to trust someone. But each time I tried, I was betrayed. I wanted to do right, but I failed at every opportunity and every attempt. Suspicion was a way of life, and alcohol was the medicine that loosened my nerves and rocked me to sleep each night. Indifference and denial was my mask, so I was blind or perhaps naive to Robbie's subtle change.

One of our business discussions was particularly painful for me. I had an unspoken attraction to a guy who worked for us, and it was established that we did not mix business with pleasure, because it was dangerous. I was the only female, and we were all close—so close that they would shower in front of me after we packaged our product at Robbie's dad's house two to three times a week.

As a boss, my cut and Robbie's was almost even, and those who worked for us were paid handsomely. However, this guy came from a large, poor family, and I enjoyed shopping for people I cared about. I would buy clothes for him each week. I felt a kinship with him, and he confided in me that he was having difficulty coping with the things he had done under Robbie's direction. He admitted that he had started snorting cocaine. That broke my heart, because one of the rules Robbie had laid down was that we don't use any of our products. My friend knew what I would say. I had to tell Robbie, because he had become a threat now. For the first and only time, I brushed my lips across his and left him on the balcony of my apartment.

I met Robbie at Seventeenth and Susquehanna for our meeting, with a heavy heart. My loyalty was to him, and there was no way to keep this from him. If he found out, I knew, the consequences would be severe. I could only ask, "Robbie, just fire him. He's my friend, don't hurt him."

I've never seen him again. I can only hope that Robbie honored my request. I didn't ask, because in the streets of Philadelphia, those questions weren't asked unless you were wearing a wire. I lived by the code of the streets. Death before dishonor. The less you know, the longer you live. Period.

I went back to my apartment, trying not to think about the guy but unable to shake the fear and sadness I saw in his eyes. I needed to swim, to rid my mind of those images. I went to the playground on Ninth Street. It was after eleven o'clock at night, so I had to scale the fence to get to the pool. I jumped in, fully clothed, and let the water ease me. I swam laps underwater for several minutes until I noticed there were other people in the pool. I climbed out, intent on leaving, and—*splash!* Some boys I knew from my block threw me back in. We splashed around and dunked each other.

When I tried to leave again, one of the boys said, "You have to kiss me on my cheek first."

I leaned in to kiss his cheek, and he turned around. His lips grazed mine.

Robbie yelled, "What the fuck are you doing?" and slammed his bat through a link in the fence.

"What?"

"What are you doing? You're around here kissing niggas while your boys are out of supplies and customers are lining up?"

"I needed to swim."

I climbed over the fence. As soon as my feet hit the ground, Robbie hit me and stretched me out.

When I came to, he was walking out of the playground and under the bridge. I vigorously shook my head to clear it and ran behind him with one thought running round and round inside my head: *My father never hit me, and no man is going to hit me after Kevin.*

I ran by him and up the four flights of steps to my apartment. He was on my heels. I flung the door open and swiftly stepped around my mom and to my bedroom closet to retrieve my pearl-handled .357. With Robbie swinging a bat and me attempting to load a gun, my mom went into hysterics.

Our partnership and friendship was over. From the back of my closet, I removed several guns, including a twelve-gauge, a bulletproof vest, and a Gucci travel bag of drugs, including heroin, crack, and powder cocaine. I also pulled out a colander, scale, and other paraphernalia. I could hear my mother's gasp before she ran a string of obscenities and unnecessary questions.

"You were selling drugs? You had drugs and guns in my house?"

To which I replied, "How do you think I paid the rent and bought so many things for you, my sisters, my daughter, and myself? Who do you think bought that car and jewelry for you? Where do I work?"

Robbie and I parted ways, and I couldn't understand what had happened between us. I was his friend and confidante, so what had changed? Then I recalled the first Mother's Day weekend that I had celebrated as a new mother. It was the Saturday before

Mother's Day, and I didn't have any plans. Robbie took me out to an expensive Chinese restaurant. I had sake with my ribs and the entire evening was a blur. I remember the ribs being exceptionally hot. I don't remember the ride home. I remember one thing and one thing only. I woke up and saw the thick curls of Robbie's hair between my legs.

I went spiraling backward through time to my childhood and felt abject terror. I took stock of my surroundings as if I was having an out-of-body experience. I recognized the room. I was in the spare bedroom of his father's apartment. As it had in the past, my body froze in panic, and I desperately wanted it to end.

In most of the consensual sex that I'd had, even if I had initiated it, my body would function properly but mentally I would want it to stop. Robbie released my legs and left the bedroom. I went to shower and brooded over why this had happened, what would happen to our friendship.

We didn't speak of it, but our friendship became strained and difficult. Our conversations were strictly business related, with long lapses of silence. We continued this way for two months until that night at the pool.

I didn't see Robbie again until he found me in South Philly when he was on the run for questioning about a murder. He explained how things weren't the same without me. There was no loyalty and trust with his new crew. Once things got hot, a couple of his new boys rolled over on him and gave incriminating statements.

Robbie was arrested several days later. To this day, my mom won't speak Robbie's name, because she believes he ruined me, destroyed my life, and crushed her dreams for me. But no—my life was ruined when the first man touched an undeveloped child's body, something I never recovered from. A piece of me died at that moment and was never resuscitated. Robbie was just like every other man in my life: came in through the front door, took something from me, and walked out the back door.

I thought that life was behind me. I thought Robbie would be the end of an abusive life. I thought wrong. As it turned out, the first man who had ever touched me without my consent would also be the last man to try.

When I was eighteen, I was at my grandmother's house. The basement was completely furnished, and I fell asleep on the bed. Sometime during the night, I felt hands on me, pulling down my pajama bottoms and my panties. I lost my mind at that moment. I kept thinking, *This is not happening! I am eighteen and no one's doing this to me again.* I fought my father off and heard him whisper, "Sorry," as he left the basement. I locked the door and couldn't shed a tear. My threshold for rage had peaked.

I lay awake all night and acknowledged that I had had enough. In the morning, I called a friend and told him what happened. His response shocked me: "What am I supposed to do about it?"

I hung up. I was so hurt, because I needed somebody to care, to share in my anger, or to listen and tell me it wasn't my fault, that it would get better. I had no positive coping skills or reinforcements. When I phoned my youngest sister, she told me something that pushed me over the edge. My father had been molesting my middle sister for years. When he couldn't perform intercourse on her, he subjected her to oral sex.

My sister! Not my sister!

I punched a dent in the wall of my grandmother's dining room. I wanted to hurt my father, but I also wanted to hurt myself when my sister said, "We couldn't tell you because you were crazy and you might've killed him. We didn't want you to hurt nobody and get in trouble."

My sisters kept it from me to protect me when the only thing I wanted to do was to protect them. In the end, I didn't protect them and they couldn't protect me. I was beyond protection.

Sheena King

To Keeva and Keiff

If I was famous and had riches untold,
every item in the world would be marked "Sold."
I'd bring you flowers, exotic and rare.
Give you the sun, the moon, unpolluted air.
Your heads would rest on clouds—fluffy, white.
You'd never know pain or darkness, only light.
Every wish and desire would be my will;
you'd never feel lonely; you'd never be ill.
A world of love songs I would raise my voice to sing.
I'd deny you nothing, give you everything.

Sheena King

My Children

Love you
'til I breathe
my last breath,
'til there's
nothing except
bones and teeth left.

Journal Entry: October 20, 2004

Lord, what is normal? What is it like to be a child and enjoy a happy family life where you aren't violated and touched and told you're not good enough? What is it like? How would it feel to be free and safe? How do we find our way back to the yellow brick road when a hand touched us and pushed us onto a detour? Is there any way we can heal and not feel? Lord, tell us what is real?

Oh God, this is so hard. Each time someone in my group breaks through and starts their healing process, I feel so much happiness for them, because the path to wholeness is necessary. But oh God, how it hurts when they hurt. When I read about what happened to them, or when they speak and share their pain, I feel so helpless. Sometimes it sends me back to being a small, weak child. Sometimes I get so angry…

Why did this happen?

CHAPTER 11

February 2014—Remembering Christmas 1990 and July 1991

From the back seat, I stared at the taillights of the vehicles in front of us. It had been a frigid, snowy winter, and banks of dirty snow, now frozen solid, lined the highway. I thought it was beautiful, tried not to stare wide-eyed, like a tourist. But it was difficult. Even the handcuffs and leg chains failed to quell my excitement.

I watched cars roll by and marveled at how different they looked from the pictures in magazine advertisements. Mouth agape, I swung my head from side to side, refusing to miss a single sign for Red Roof Inn, Perkins Family Restaurant, Motel 6, or Super 8, along with fast food establishments I was familiar with: McDonald's, Wendy's, and Arby's.

Different thoughts struggled with each other for predominance:

FNB! That was my bank.

Wow, these houses look the same in real life as all those suburban houses I see on the news every night.

Where are the Black people?

Some of these Christmas decorations are lovely.

Oh God! I can see people through that window! I bet their house is warm and filled with love.

Although my thoughts tumbled one over the other like children at play, the last led me backward, to the preceding months, and to events that changed the course of my life forever.

❦

It was another cold day in 1990, weeks before Christmas. "Oh, Santa Claus." I smiled down at my daughter clad in a bright-pink snow suit, pink-and-white hat with matching gloves, and designer boots.

"I see him, baby, but I'm your Santa Claus," I replied as we walked hand in hand to the supermarket in the early evening. We oohed and aahed at every beautifully decorated house.

"I want to live in that house," my daughter said. She wouldn't be two years old until December 19, but she already knew what she wanted.

"We will, baby. I promise."

❦

Riding in the back of the van, in awe of all that I was missing, of all that I had taken for granted, my heart was still heavy. I hadn't kept that promise to my baby. She wanted a big, bright, warm house, full of love—my love, raising her to become the woman that she would become anyway, even without my being there. I looked down at my cuffed hands resting on my breasts while the heart behind them silently broke into a million pieces for the millionth time over the pain I was causing my children. I prayed quietly, "Lord, don't let me survive this surgery."

Hours later, the anesthesia wore off. I opened my eyes and angrily asked, "God, why didn't you let me die on the table? Anything would be better than this existence." My uterus wasn't the only thing I was without. I had lost my desire to live. What was the point? I didn't deserve to live. I was just wasting breath.

The painkillers coursing through my veins via the IV drip rocked me back to sleep. When I returned again to consciousness, I could barely move, because the pain was excruciating. I desperately needed to urinate, but my body couldn't expel it without the assistance of a catheter. The ride back to the prison infirmary was a blur. I slept through most of it.

I was awakened by a nurse emptying the blue urine from the catheter. For a brief disoriented moment, I thought I was a Smurf. It hurt to laugh. Again, I asked God, "Why did you let me live?" Distractedly, I wondered if God was tired of me asking the same question. I had been asking it for years—more than once, like now, as a heartfelt plea.

❦

"Summertime" by DJ Jazzy Jeff and the Fresh Prince was playing on the radio. It was a huge hit, so it played frequently, pumping through the speakers of passing cars while I sat on the steps of my apartment building at Seventh and Kennedy in the Northwest section of Washington, DC. It was a warm day in July of '91. The sun reflected off the freshly washed cars as they rode by. My copper-colored legs were turning the burnt red-brown that I hate, and the buttons on my shorts were getting snug. I was five months pregnant with my son.

I rapped along with the Fresh Prince until he mentioned "the Plateau," a section of Fairmont Park that I used to visit, and I was hit hard by nostalgia, longing, homesickness. I wanted to die. I deserved to die. How could I enjoy the warmth of the sun on my strap-sandaled feet when I had taken the life of someone I didn't know, who had never done anything to me, who deserved to be alive, basking in the sun today with her children?

I knew there was a strong possibility that my mom's phone was tapped, but I needed to tell her goodbye. So instead of using the house phone, I walked across the street and made my call at the phone booth in front of the small Black-owned corner store. I could hear my daughter's voice in the background, crying for me. I needed my daughter. I was distracted by the sound of her voice. I tried to focus on the anguish I heard in my mother's voice. She was saying something about someone spray-painting "Killer" on the front door.

Each word caused me to sink deeper into depression, reinforcing the belief that their lives would be better without me. Her voice tightened when she said, "Some guys have been coming to the house asking for you and driving slow, following your sisters to school."

"Mom, please—you have to move."

Before I committed one of the most heinous acts against another human being, I pleaded with my mom the same way, except that I admitted to her that I was in over my head. Just as she had then, she stubbornly refused again now: "Nobody's running me out of my house." (The first time she had said, "I have a gun, so nobody is making me leave.") She didn't mention the gun this time, because it was gone, and the receipt from its purchase had been evidence used to obtain a search and arrest warrant for me. I decided to postpone my death until my family was safe.

I had believed Reggie some months earlier when he threatened to have my family killed if I didn't follow his instructions. It didn't dawn on me then, not until later when I listened to my mother, that my loved ones would still not be safe because I was a witness against him.

"Mom, I can't live like this. I thought if I left then you and my family would be safe until I could figure out what to do."

"Do you want to turn yourself in?"

"I don't want to have my baby in jail, but I need to do something. I keep having dreams about it, and I feel like shit for what I did."

"Your sister's lawyer wants to talk to you."

I agreed to talk with him. I was tired of running from what I had done, those I had done it for, and their threats. I was tired of living. But taking my own life would end my son's too, and I had already taken and ruined too much.

The next day, I talked to my sister's attorney, who said, "I think it's best if you turn yourself in. You can come to my office and together we'll meet with the district attorney. We can offer you protection."

"Can you protect my family?"

"No, that protection only extends to you for your testimony."

"But they are after my family. They're terrorizing them! I don't care about protection for me. I'm not afraid! I need my daughter, my sisters, and my mom to be safe."

"I can't promise that."

I hung up, then roamed the streets of DC and the surrounding areas of Maryland talking to a God who didn't answer until I told myself that I probably wasn't worthy of an answer. I cooked food that I couldn't eat, lay across the bed yet didn't sleep.

My friend John was in the Navy, stationed in Bethesda, Maryland. I went to visit him and seek advice. "Turn yourself in," he said. I agreed, kissed him goodbye, and returned to Philadelphia.

Needless to say, my family members weren't happy. It had taken a considerable amount of money, time, planning, and other resources to get me out of state. Now I was back, and speaking nonsense as far as my grandmother was concerned.

"Turn yourself in? It's the police's job to arrest you, so let them find you!"

They did, in March 1992.

The homicide detectives allowed me to place my beautiful four-month-old son in my grandmother's arms after they let me call her to come get him and my belongings. I was escorted to their waiting car and taken to the central booking facility, called the "Round House," for the first and last time, then sat in PICC, the Philadelphia Industrial Correctional Center, without bail until my sentencing in December 1993.

I stared at the taillights of the vehicles in front of the transport van. I looked at the banks of frozen, dirty snow and the back of the sign that said "Philadelphia." That was the last time I would see the city of my birth.

Thelma Nichols

Sometimes...

We see our dreams come true ... sometimes.
We succeed in everything we do ... sometimes.
We smile and really feel good ... sometimes.
But are we true to our hearts?
Sometimes.

Do we give it our all and say to hell with it if we fall?
Sometimes.

Love makes everything alright (right) huh … sometimes…
I'll forget about their wicked ways,
The way they hurt me,
The price my soul had to pay … sometimes.
And the peaceful feeling will come
I'll feel safe and not alone … sometimes.
I'll even look at them and feel nothing … sometimes.

Yeah, well, when will sometimes be my time
For all time?

Yeah, I know … sometimes.

❦

Journal Entry: June 27, 1998

I can remember her anger, pain, and angry words. I can see her so clearly, and I can feel each word that she spoke. I can barely envision the girl that I was, but I can see it all through a haze. I need to talk to her about it before I can go further. I need to kick it with her and find out why she took him back in—why she didn't believe me when I told her what happened in the bathroom with my father. I need to tell her the truth about Jeff, because I need us to be real and close like we used to be. I need her to realize that my fears for my peeps are very real, and she has to see why. I don't want to have to keep stuffing what happened into a closet. When I think of it and feel anger, I need to express it—not like I have in the past by putting her on the defensive and feeling her anger and cutting words, not to push past it like I don't have a right to be angry, but to feel it, tell her what I feel about it, and let it dissipate in its own time.

I love my mom. I love my family, especially my babies. I just want to go home and for once in my life feel contentment, unconcealed joy, and true happiness. Like Mary J. Blige said in her song, "I just wanna be happy."

CHAPTER 12

March 1992

When I was transported to Eighth and Race Streets and shambled through the receiving doors of PICC, I was petrified. Like most teenagers from the inner city, I thought I was fearless, invincible. You had to be when you were selling drugs and could easily be robbed and murdered. Even if you were afraid, you had to conceal it under a mask of false bravado.

When I needed to carry drugs from one section of North Philly to another, or more guns in a duffel bag with a twelve-gauge strapped across my back under a long leather coat, I couldn't show fear. When the barrel of a gun was shakily pointed at my face by wild-eyed young boys demanding, "Take off your fucking jewelry and hand over your money," I couldn't quake in terror. I learned to live behind the mask. I learned to open my eyes in the face of fear but to close them tightly when I wanted to forget.

But these things that I had learned in the streets were quickly lost to me when I was stripped of my expensive clothes, my shoes, my flashy jewelry, and watched it all being itemized, tagged, and set aside for my mother to pick up. My mask was stripped away as I was ordered to strip naked in front of a female guard and shampoo my hair for lice while my body was inspected for tattoos and distinguishing marks.

Then I was escorted to a quarantine cell, where I would remain for twenty-three hours a day until I was medically cleared. I thought I would cry. I couldn't. Years spent denying myself had prevented me from being able to, until the numbness wore off. After three days, I realized that my maternal grandmother's words had turned out to be prophetic: I was in prison. Worst of all, I was in prison for murder.

Prison wasn't a place I had ever envisioned myself ending up when I was a small child, before a man's hands altered my path. But I wouldn't allow myself to dwell on this at that moment, because I didn't see that it had any relevance. I couldn't understand how any chain of events had led me down this road of incredible, unbelievable destruction. I couldn't see it then.

What I could see was jumping double Dutch, and then jumping at the sound of bullets until it was so commonplace that it had become like background music as we played hopscotch. I could also see myself at age thirteen, being unable to stay asleep. I looked out the window at the dark sky and thought of making a wish to the stars. I glanced around, pondering what to wish for, when I spotted a tall, dark-skinned man I hadn't seen before. Where had he come from? Was he a heroin addict? Why was he just sitting there on the fence rail with that long coat on?

I watched him look around nervously, tapping his right foot repeatedly without rhythm. It seemed as if I watched him for an hour, but in reality it was only several minutes later when two men walked up and shot him once. I saw his body fall to the side and to the ground. Then one of the men shot him in his forehead. I jumped back from the window.

When I found the courage, or enough curiosity, I stole another peek, long enough to note that the two men were gone and the stranger was on the ground, not moving. Hearing about or seeing someone shot was not shocking in the ghetto. Seeing detectives investigate or witnesses coming forward in the Richard Allen projects would have been surprising, however. This time there were no surprises. I never learned who the stranger was, except that he had recently been released from jail and had ratted on some people.

As weird as it may seem, I wasn't frightened of the streets. I was, however, of what wasn't yet known to me when I was medically cleared and released to the general population.

"Damn, you pretty. Come here, little girl!"

I kept my head down and walked briskly to one of the four phones lining the wall near the correctional officers' station.

"Mom, they're going to rape me," I whispered into the phone while stealing glances at the woman who had called me. Her voice was husky and deep. Her close-cropped hair, which had been curled to the back, was coarse. So was the hair that sprouted from her chin.

Where am I?

"What?" my mother shouted.

"These dykes in here are going to rape me."

"What?! Not you, big billy badass," she said, laughing. My mother had a way with words. But she was right. I talked to my daughter too, then put my mask back on.

I had heard the stories about jail and had seen a few movies. So I prepared myself. No one was taking anything from me without a fight. I walked over to the table where the bearded woman and three other aggressive-looking females were playing pinochle and said, "My name is not 'girl' and there is nothing little about me!" Then I went to my cell to get changed for a shower.

Those movies turned out to be just that—movies. No one was raped while I was in PICC, including me.

This prison, I learned, was a small neighborhood within a city. There were no limits. Drugs flowed freely, and for a moment, almost two years, I forgot where I was—as if I had never stopped being the street hustler I had been before. I was doing what I had been taught to do: sex and selling drugs.

There were inmates who worked "outside," and in exchange for a small fee they would sneak my packages back into the prison. A friend or business associate would tightly wrap a small package of drugs into a tubelike shape and place it inside a condom or wrap it in plastic and leave it just outside the entrance to the prison in a trash can that was always there. The returning worker would retrieve it from the trash can, go into the bathroom near the entrance doors, conceal it on or in her body before being patted down, and then bring it to the cell block.

I sold cocaine, heroin, marijuana, and an assortment of pills, until one day a package that was too large became lodged inside someone. The worst gynecologist is an untrained inmate. A friend helped to remove the package, but there was blood everywhere. So I had to change tactics. Officers were also always willing to bring contraband in for a small fee, and one of them had become a customer as well.

❦

The fear I had experienced on entering PICC had by now vanished. But it swiftly returned when the Philadelphia sheriff's van drove through the gates of the State Correctional Institution (SCI) at Muncy, to the admissions building.

The strip search, shampoo, shower, and recording of tattoos and distinguishing marks were expected. What I didn't expect was the beauty of the grounds and the snow-covered mountains in the background. But I soon found out that the beauty was only external—skin deep, as with a beautiful woman who is also bitter, cold, and dead on the inside.

The grounds are swept clean, the grass mowed, trees trimmed. During spring and summer, colorful flowers brighten the lawn around every housing unit. That's the outside. But the reality is the opposite: Anything that makes you feel human, or like a woman, is explicitly forbidden or else taken away. Many of your fellow inmates are unnecessarily cruel and vindictive. To thrive in this place, even just to survive, is a test of will and determination.

Then there is the ominous presence of death that surrounds the prison—as if the Angel himself had his own private cell, just down the corridor. As I've begun to age and develop health problems like fibroids, possible cervical cancer, and high blood pressure, I am reminded of the one thing I never feared when I was out on the street: dying.

When I had been at SCI Muncy for a few months, I was called to the counselor's office. He explained that a more experienced woman serving a life sentence always met with and talked to the "new lifers" to help in the acceptance and transition period. I looked at her; she smiled; I frowned. I was twenty-one; she looked to be in her forties. I am Black; she was white. I am from the hood; she clearly was not.

What can this woman tell me about accepting the near impossible? I wondered. I don't remember anything she said except this: "Never think about dying in here."

To myself I responded, *Who thinks about that?!*

I was twenty-one. I didn't think about dying in here or anywhere else, and I was irritated that she would say such a thing to me. She gave me nothing to look forward to, which was depressing. I would have to figure out how to do my time on my own, with the observational skills that had served me my entire life.

But aging and death surrounded me. I would frequently play pinochle with older lifers whom I respected—Peachie, Roddy, and Meechie. They and a few others would become the women I learned from. During the game, they would complain about ailments that plagued them. It was always their knees, their backs, arthritis in their hands. There was always something. Quietly I would be annoyed, because I couldn't relate. I was young, strong, and physically healthy. I sought friends who were closer to my own age, because it was hard to hear how vibrant and active these older women had once been while now they lived through chronic and debilitating pain. It was more than I could deal with.

In recent years, however, I'm reminded of those card games with my "old heads" because my younger friends from those days—Dierdre, Karen, Terri, and Tamika—are now the old heads to the twenty-year-olds. We complain to them about our slowly failing bodies as we reminisce about our glory years as younger, much more active and able-bodied women. It would be a funny twist on getting older, except that it isn't. It's a sad thing to be aging in prison. Our conversations used to center on "when I go home," what we were going to wear or eat, the places we wanted to go. Now I look into the eyes of these women I grew up with and I see my own pain and fear reflected back to me in their eyes. I have to look away.

Each of us has soaked the shoulders of the others as we've cried over the death of a loved one: Terri's greatly cherished grandmother, Dierdre's aunt and father, Karen's parents and oldest brother, my mother's only sister, Belle, and the only man she ever loved, my Uncle Pete. And none of us thought about her own mortality until our old heads started dying around us—like Peachie, who was beloved by everyone in this place, inmates and guards alike.

And then there was Najah. Her passing was different for me. With Peachie, I was devastated and felt abandoned by a member of my immediate family. She raised me, supported me, believed in me, and always saw more in me than I saw in myself. If she was sick, you wouldn't know it, because she rarely talked about herself. Her concern was for the world and for the eventual freedom of lifers in general. Literally, I was talking to her one day about how she'd live her life when she went home, and two days later, after a visit with friends, she was gone.

With Najah, on the other hand, I felt helpless, useless. She was my roommate and so, in a matter of months, I watched up close as she changed from a curvaceous, funny, attractive woman to one who was dangerously thin and frail, racked with pain every day and every night. She couldn't eat, and when she did she couldn't keep it down. She made weekly trips to the infirmary and was taken frequently to Geisinger and Williamsport hospitals for tests. The diagnosis was inconclusive, so the medical staff decided that it was "all in her head." But they would soon find it was cancer instead. It killed her painfully, and slowly.

It's strange the things that remain with you after someone has gone. For instance, whenever I see *Star Trek* on the TV guide I think of Peachie, and every Monday and Friday, without fail, I'm reminded of how much Najah loved wrestling and John Cena. She watched it religiously, was as passionate about it as she was about Islam and her family. Her animated descriptions of the characters compelled me to watch it with her, because, for that moment, she was happy and her pain seemed to subside.

I haven't watched it since.

Najah and I were roommates when I was released from the infirmary after my hysterectomy. With both of us in physical pain, there was very little either of us could do for the other. This was an extremely depressing time for me. My body healed much faster than my mind. I was in the beginning stages of a breakup from a long-term relationship, so I was grieving the absence of that other significant person in my life and the absence of my uterus at the same time. Nevertheless, after Najah's passing I felt as if I could have done more to ease her discomfort. I could have spoken to the administration more than once so she could receive the medical attention she needed.

It frightens me to watch my elders' skin sag and their quick-paced walk slow to a crawl, some even requiring the aid of canes and wheelchairs. It depresses me that Terri and Dierdre needed back surgeries, that Karen is frightened and wondering how long she has to live because of multiple medical complications. We grew up in Muncy together, and their mortality is a testament to my own. So we try not to talk about it as we watch and cry while our friends and associates die around us.

No one wants to die alone and in prison. But it's our reality, and we fear it.

❦

Journal Entry: June 1, 2001

I was just reading the Twenty-Third Psalm. I remembered how I was reciting it while walking down the hall to the courtroom. By the time I came to the end of the verse I was outside the doors of the courtroom and I knew! I said, "I'm going to get life." I resigned myself to it.

The days leading up to my sentencing it seemed likely to go either way. I thought maybe five, ten, any and everything. Maybe God was telling me before I received my sentence, because I hadn't actually believed it when I was periodically told by inmates that I would get life. At any rate, God told me. I didn't want it but He prepared me for it.

Prepared? You can never prepare for those words. You can never prepare yourself, those whom you love and who love you in return. You can't reshuffle the deck.

I can write my story but I can't rewrite my life.

❦

Terri Harper

Sharin' My Pain

How do you handle the sorrow…
When once again, for someone you love **and** admire,
there is no tomorrow?
Your inclination, no matter how wrong, is to ask, "Why?"
And I'm trying…
To hold tight and not give in to the terrible sadness I feel inside.
It was just yesterday she asked me to do her a favor
but didn't have time to explain.
I just knew a note would follow the request,
but it was all in vain.
For God had a Plan, and Only He knew Best
What was a hope, a dream, a wish for the rest.
Now those left to mourn have but memories…
Some in abundance … some powerful, but few.
The majority of mine were formed over bread, wings, and cookies
… a battle or two.
She embodied intelligence—a quotient unmatched here.
And despite the path realized, the seemingly long road ahead,
death wasn't a spoken fear.
She chose to live each day, giving, supporting, and educating any
who'd let her gift in.
Being blessed to be a part of her inner circle was as sweet as sin.
A Mentor, a Friend, a Confidante…
A Daughter, a Sister, a Surrogate, an Aunt…
Loyal, Honest, Funny, Ready, Deserving…
Time on this earth ran out for her, and that's unnerving.
But from this Great Loss of one who truly impacted
just about half of my life
I Will **not** give up the Fight!!
Dear God, I beseech Thee,
Please grant Heaven to our dear departed Peachie.

CHAPTER 13

January 1994

While I was in the County, I saw my family every week, most times twice a week. I called home every day. I had been in SCI Muncy for a month and hadn't received mail from anyone. I hadn't made a phone call, because Mom didn't have collect on her phone. Never in my life had I felt such loneliness.

The hay fever that has plagued me since I was a child had worsened in the mountain air. I checked my skin for bugs. Zero, but the itch persisted. I scratched until I bled. I couldn't breathe in this place. *It must be my bronchitis,* I thought. I needed to ask my mom. She was a nurse. She'd know the answer. But I couldn't call her. *Shit!* I requested to see a doctor.

"You'll see the PA."

"PA?" I asked.

"Yeah, the physician's assistant, King."

"King?" I hadn't gotten used to being called by my last name. In PICC, they referred to us by our first names, and they didn't speak to me as though pronouncing my name left a nasty taste in their mouths.

The PA said, "It's just anxiety. Take Ativan at number four med line."

"Anxiety, what do you mean?"

"A-N-X-I-E-T-Y." He spoke slowly, as if I didn't understand the word.

"I heard what you said, but I have hay fever and bronchitis, both of which I was born with. I need Visine because my eyes are sealed shut every morning, and I need Benadryl. I also need a vaporizer for my bronchitis."

He laughed loud and long, as if I'd made a crude joke. "You won't get a vaporizer here. And I said it's anxiety."

I took the proffered medication card from his hand. That night, I walked to the infirmary, to med line, and swallowed the pill. I slept until the evening of the following day. I don't remember waking up for count, the several-times-a-day process where they come around to make sure we are all in our cells where we belong. I didn't go to med line again for that pill. I suffered in silence.

Spiritually, I believe unequivocally that our times are in God's hands, that He is the deciding factor for when we live and die. However, my feelings of inadequacy and incompetence persist. Coupled with these feelings is an underlying depression. As with every human being, depression is not foreign to me. But in 2014, the length of time during which I remained depressed began to trouble me. As a spiritual woman and an optimistic Sagittarius, I normally buoy myself out of bouts of depression or negative emotions quickly. Most of the time I am able to. But when, more recently, the insomnia, weight loss, and thinning hair began to worry me and my closest friends, I sought help from a very compassionate yet eccentric psychologist named Howard. He referred me to a psychiatrist who, in turn, prescribed Zoloft.

Independently even of my previous brief experience with Ativan, I dreaded the use of psychotropic medications. My sister, Nena, suffers from schizophrenia but refuses her medication because it quiets the voices. To her, the voice is from God and she wants to hear it, so she drinks excessively instead. I don't quite understand her rationale, but then I also don't understand the effects psychotropic medications have on the brain. What I do know is what I see of their effect on other women prisoners.

Some of these women were "normal" years ago. Now, most days, I feel as if I'm in Center City, Philadelphia. There's the chubby Latina lady who speaks little English, except to ask for a cigarette while she's smoking one already. The pockets of her coat have holes created by burns from the lit cigarettes that she stuffs in them as she mumbles to herself and spits on the floor of the infirmary while standing in line to receive her medications.

There's Robin, who slicks her short hair to the back with fingers moistened by spit. One day she whipped open her coat. She had pairs of seemingly new socks pinned to the lining. We were in the yard. "Do you wanna buy some socks?"

"What? No!"

"Well, do you wanna buy some soap?" She had a few bars in her pocket.

"No, Robin, I need some cigarettes."

I looked around for the officer and took a step closer to my Kaya, my friend and intimate companion. For a moment, I felt like I was on the street and about to be robbed. But she walked away, cursing her misfortune.

Often I ask myself, "Where am I?"—especially when I see Shamika, who many have claimed was not this way at home or when she arrived here. I can attest to the latter. But now I hear her talk to trees, to doors, to inanimate objects, even to the sky. In the meal line, she'll dance by herself or make loud, outlandish claims that an unnamed someone wants to see her naked. Shamika is a "Z-code," meaning she cannot be housed with anyone else. This is a blessing, because anyone unlucky enough to live with her would be at her mercy. Everyone gives her a wide berth and tries to avoid conversations or direct eye contact—just like in the streets.

Everyone assumed Ebony was basically harmless. Sure, in the dead of winter she might strip down to her pants and T-shirt and run at top speed around the track in the yard, or shake and gyrate her hips to a song that only she can hear. But no one expected her to grab a male correctional officer's crotch.

So when I was offered psychotropic medication, I considered the women around me. I discussed my apprehension and shared with the psychiatrist my theory of how psych drugs make "normal" people insane. She assured me that my fears were unfounded and convinced me to try it. I did—for a week of feeling loopy and fatigued. I wasn't so easily agitated, but decided it's not for me. I will suffer through the depression and the awareness of my own mortality with a heavy heart but a clear head. My resolve was reinforced by a woman barking like a dog.

Walking back to the housing unit from dinner, I heard raised voices, so I craned my neck to see through the crowd. A woman of about five feet, nine inches was vehemently barking in another inmate's face. I thought she was going to bite her. I leaned in close to Kaya and refused to walk any closer to that bizarre scene until a sergeant intervened to speak to this woman in soothing tones. I thought about the first time I'd seen her. It was in May 2014, and I was working in the admissions building for the nurse. Although her hair was dyed multicolored—reminiscent of a tall, light-skinned, 240-pound Rainbow Brite doll—she was very pleasant and soft-spoken. She answered the nurse's questions with humor and intelligence. They shared a laugh about her mishap with dying her hair. She didn't growl. She wasn't barking. She didn't scream and pound on walls like she'd been doing lately.

So what happens to these women? No one can give me a clear and concise answer. I choose, therefore, to avoid the psych drugs.

I didn't have a roommate yet. At mail call, I tried not to appear anxious, so I stayed on my assigned top bunk while listening to the soft whisper of envelopes being slid under doors. *Please, God. Please.* I prayed silently. The officer walked past my door. I cried into my pillow, asking God why I hadn't heard from my family. *Don't they love me? Does anyone care? I'm up here, miles away from home and they've forgotten me. I'm alone. Please, God, let me hear from my family.*

I didn't expect an answer. I cried myself to sleep and slept peacefully through the night.

I don't know how long I slept, but I woke up with a distinct feeling that someone was embracing me. *I smell roses,* I thought. It felt comforting, and I smelled roses, clearly. I jumped from the bed, flung the window up, and looked out. The ground was still frozen. There was no sign of roses or any flowers, not even grass.

"Why do I smell roses?" I muttered. I stood there shivering in stunned bewilderment until I realized I was freezing and closed the window. For several seconds, I could still smell the roses until the scent slowly faded. I heard a sound and turned to see the officer pushing envelope after envelope under my door. I couldn't believe it. There were letters, cards, even pictures, with return addresses from my mom, my sisters, grandmothers, aunts, uncles, cousins—and a card from my children, which I opened first. I could barely contain my joy.

But there was something I had to do before anything else. I sank to my knees and thanked God. Intuitively I sensed that the roses, the feeling of comfort and contentment, and this outpouring of love and support from my family came from Him. This time He had answered my prayers. It created a love and curiosity in me for a God I had not known—the God who did not protect me when I was a child. Instinctively I felt that God was real. Something inside me changed that day, and I knew that no matter what challenges I faced—the hurt, the remorse, the pain and guilt I felt—I could get through this.

I would be lying if I said that everything improved from that moment on. It didn't. My relationship with God, my faith and trust in God, was challenged. I wrestled; I complained; I turned my back on more occasions than I care to remember. The only thing that's remained solid from that cold day in 1994 to this humid one as I write these lines in 2014 was my belief that God is real. I find that what you call Him doesn't matter (at least not for me): Lord, God, Jesus, Jehovah, Allah, or Shiva, as long as you call Him.

Because of my belief in God, and in the importance of doctrine, I've learned from several religions. I struggled mightily with my sexuality. I reasoned that being molested made me this way, but I needed to be honest with myself. I lay awake one night and searched my memory while I tossed and turned on the bed, hoping the creaking springs didn't disturb my roommate as she slept on the bunk beneath me. I had always been attracted to women. I remembered my first time, with Lil, was prior to the molestation.

It pained me to have no excuse for my lesbianism. I wanted to blame it on something else, hoping I might be "cured" if I had a good man—the way religious literature told me I could. The truth was difficult to accept. I prayed hard to be rid of my attraction to the same sex. I pleaded to be "normal." I refused to be in relationships and carried my Bible everywhere as some sort of amulet to ward off my own desires. It worked for almost a year.

Ironically, the woman who proved to be stronger than my amulet was as involved in the church as I was and knew her Bible as well as I did—though later I would obtain an associate's degree in religious studies. Charlotta and I were together for seven years, and through her I learned a great deal about myself, about relationships that weren't based on sex, about how to truly be a friend. The battle with my sexuality ended as I came to an acceptance of self.

The hardest battles are the ones we wage within ourselves. They are also our greatest victories. If, in God's eyes, my sexual preference is an abomination, as so many religions claim, then He is the one I will answer to when it's time.

Personally, I see no difference between heterosexual relationships and same-sex relationships. So why the judgment? I've seen female officers hiding black eyes—that their husbands caused—behind large sunglasses, just as I've hidden my own black eye caused by an angry female ex-partner. I listen to male officers talk about how much they love their wives or girlfriends and the gifts they have purchased for their spouses for Valentine's Day or Mother's Day. As prisoners, we discuss the gifts we are planning to give or those we've received from our partners. We are just as happy and sentimental.

Infidelity is also the same, and as difficult to keep secret. Male officers cheat on their wives with female coworkers and female inmates. Female officers cheat on their husbands or boyfriends with male officers and female inmates. Female inmates cheat on their partners with officers, roommates, their girlfriends' best friends. There's an old saying: "The closest gets the mostest." And it's true for this environment regardless if you clock out after eight hours or have been confined here by a judge. It's all the same. The difference is in the individual.

Some intimate relationships are still going strong after decades of walking in this same circle, with no real way for two people to get away from each other. Many friendships have lasted just as long, if not longer. The capacity for love is the greatest gift. So what makes it wrong? What people do with it becomes the problem—not who you love ... but how you love.

Journal Entry: September 8, 2011

"If she sees how much I'm hurting she'll take me back for sure." A line from a song by the Script brings me back to thoughts I've been having about love, loss, and relationships: If she sees him hurting it won't matter, if she's done with him.

I think about how Fran is with Shamia now and doesn't even see Kristen, who's at the point of contemplating suicide. I see Kwanna writing novel-length letters to my best friend Dierdre (Deej), trying not to let her pain show when we see her.

I see the hurt. I also see the excitement and joy of newfound love. It's nice and it's cute, but my emotions tend to be with those who are hurting, because I remember what it is like to not be over someone, how difficult it was to accept that she no longer wanted me. Rejection is a hard pill to swallow, as is abandonment. I remember looking for any sign that she still wanted me, was still in love with me even though her words and actions indicated the opposite. Years later, I had to finally accept that the only part of me she still desired was my sex. So I tried to use sex to bring her love back, but I couldn't do it in the end because that never works. Sex is just sex—a momentary fulfillment, or a spiritual uniting if love is involved. But that's all it is.

I think about how Deej never really wanted Kwanna, was just experimenting. I think about my new love and how she's so involved for now. *But aren't they all? I'm so fed up with what I see on talk shows like* Maury *and* Jerry *and when I look around me. Relationships don't last, and there always seems to be infidelity or a leftover love forced to hold together the pieces of her broken heart.*

I tend to pull back from Kaya because I don't want the broken heart again, but she notices me doing it. I was safer alone—maybe not happy, but safe. Yet doesn't living life require taking some risks?

I don't really know the reasons behind Toni's suicide attempt, but I believe she really wants to die. It wasn't just a need for attention. She really wants to end this, and I can understand that. When you're serving a never-ending life sentence with no hope—because you've exhausted the appeal process and because commutation is a possibility in name only—what do you have? Sadly, you have the love that you can find here, inside this prison. When it is unrequited, the only thing left is the emptiness.

Sheena King

Untitled No. 1

I stand alone in my silence.
I hear the sound of glass
shattering, while
I feel a pinching in my chest, like a
dagger through the soft tissue.
The pain expands across the band
of my breast, like fire through wild brush—
I release a howl.
If I dare to look down, I
am certain that I will see
pieces of me,
of my heart,
cascading to the ground like fine
sand from an hourglass.
Grainy reminders of the hour
you crushed my heart
and turned my future into my past.

Sheena King

Kaya

When I wasn't looking I stumbled and you found me.
Full of intelligence, wisdom, vitality.
Your skill brought back to life what had died.
I was broken, picking up pieces, sorting through lies.
I had given up on love, placed my focus on self—
not wanting sport or a mate to endanger my health.
I turned my back on my first love and even put down my pen.
Couldn't write another poem, found no words to begin.
I had plans for solitude, a quiet reclusive life.
No need for a companion, certainly not a wife.
But you intruded on my space, fueled by desire.
Your persistence weakened me, set my soul afire.
You wouldn't be denied, you shot down my objections,
weren't fazed by excuses, reasons, or rejections.
When I wasn't looking, you stole my heart and head,
changed me, rewrote my story: just as you said.

Journal Entry: October 11, 2011

When reading about the Holy Spirit in my Our Daily Bread *devotional, I thought about the way the Holy Spirit dwells in Christians to change behavior and make humans Christlike. It seems to be a theme in religions. In Buddhism, the goal is enlightenment, a higher form of consciousness, Karma, reaching a higher level of learning with each life. In Islam, discipline is practiced to raise a person to a higher level, to submit, to become humble, to live modestly. With five obligatory prayers every day and a month of fasting, the focus is on Allah, just as prayer and the Holy Spirit puts the focus on Jesus for Christians. In Eastern religions, through mysticism and meditation, practitioners focus on something higher than themselves. There's a common thread that runs through all religions. It's almost as if the basic foundation was the same and God isn't greatly concerned about the religious or the religions per se. It's a focus on Him, on something higher than yourself, an ability to see our own smallness in the larger picture.*

CHAPTER 14

April 1998

In 1993, when I arrived, the population of SCI Muncy was just over 600 inmates. As I write this, in 2014, there are over 1,500 women incarcerated here. Now, as it was then, many of them have an incredibly low sense of self-esteem, false bravado, codependency, and a deep, undeniable yearning for love and acceptance. After I had been in Muncy for five years, trying to adjust, change my behavior, grow in wisdom, and figure out who I needed to be, I volunteered to participate in the "House of Hope," an intensive inpatient therapeutic community for survivors of domestic violence and sexual abuse. There I found twenty-five of the women I just described. I was the twenty-sixth.

I was fiercely private. The last thing I wanted to do was talk about my life. There was no pressure, but we were all subtly encouraged by Joan Segar, the staff counselor for abuse. In the safe confines of the group room where we met once a week, Joan freely shared her life of molestation as a child and her physically abusive relationships.

Living in this building was a contrast to the rest of SCI Muncy. We were discussing our past, but when I walked out of the door to go to my work detail, meals, or the recreational yard, these stories were being lived out by others. It was no secret that inmates were having sex with guards for cigarettes, just as they had at PICC. By law this is considered rape, because guards are in a position of power. In addition to sex, traded for so little, it was common enough to go to the yard and see another woman poorly concealing a black eye with sunglasses because she'd had a fight with her girlfriend.

All of that was forgotten in the group room, where relationships were discouraged because of the distraction they create when you are trying to focus on yourself and heal. That didn't stop me, however, because I felt a new fear—a fear of actually changing. Who or what would I become?

Over time, I have discovered that I learn more about myself through relationships than from any other tactic, self-help book, or teacher. I had major trust issues. So it was necessary to view myself and to increase my self-esteem through the acceptance I received from someone else who cared for me. My unconscious rationale was that she saw the real Sheena. She read my poems and knew what I truly felt about myself, so maybe she could envision who I would become if I changed. I didn't possess the foresight to do it on my own. I needed a gentle push to encourage me to step into and through my fear of the unknown.

I was afraid again, afraid of what I was feeling as I listened to these women. I was feeling enraged at what had happened to me as a child, also at the things these women had endured. At one point, I turned that rage on my girlfriend: "Listen, you stupid-ass bitch, why can't you get it? I don't want your tall bald-head ass! You're loud. You bitch too much and you have no class. Just leave me the fuck alone."

The words spewed from my mouth with so much force and venom and spittle that tears instantly clouded her vision. Her head shot back, like the words were a physical blow. I felt satisfied—for the moment. I knew I was wrong but I couldn't control myself, and this continued daily for a month.

During a group session some days later, one of the participants shared the story of her abusive relationship with another woman, and I realized that I was also an abuser. How could I have treated Charlotta so cruelly, especially when she was trying to heal from her own abusive past? I apologized to her, thanked her for standing beside me, and vowed never to mistreat her or anyone else again.

"You were purposely trying to hurt me because you are hurting and you don't realize it," she replied. "I get it, because I've been there. I'm not giving up on you. Just stop lying to yourself, pretending you are fine and have it all together when you don't—or you won't get better."

She was right. I had been in the House of Hope for six weeks when Charlotta graduated and moved out. We remain friends to this day.

Sitting in the yard on a beautiful day in May, I finally told someone about my life. When I saw the acceptance and understanding in her eyes as we cried together, my fear of being judged if I told people, and my abject terror in the face of the person I might become, disappeared.

In group sessions, I finally talked, and instead of sitting with my arms crossed over my chest, only hearing the words spoken by others, I actually started listening. I cried and learned to care deeply about these women. When I graduated from the House of Hope on September 14, 1998, I promised the program director, Melinda, that if she ever needed me to come back and help, or just speak about how the experience changed me and changed my life, I wouldn't hesitate.

I didn't think she would take me up on that offer, because I had stuttered through the presentation of my "life-line"—a timeline that the House of Hope requires of each participant, written as a graph with the low points in your life marked, such as the first time I was molested and the sexual assaults, along with the high points, such as the birth of my children. I had also clumsily displayed my "Clothesline Project" T-shirt, an opportunity we were given to artistically express our journeys from victim to survivor. Paint, brushes, markers, glitter, glue, and stencils were made available, and each of us was allotted as much time as we needed to complete the project.

My creativity, however, has always been expressed by putting my heart on paper through words. So I did that once again by creating a T-shirt that said "Stop the Hand That Kills Us" and then tracing my own hand. There were many talented broken women who invented vivid and disturbing visual images. Some, in startling detail, painted a picture that mere words could not reproduce. These T-shirts were then hung with wooden clothespins on lines throughout the entire building, including the group room.

In October, for Domestic Violence Awareness Month, handpicked T-shirts were exhibited in the General Population Library of the prison. Twenty or thirty were chosen and, to my surprise, mine was one of them. I could not have foreseen, during the graduation ceremony, that this would happen, just as I hadn't imagined that Mrs. Melinda would actually accept my offer to help. But she did exactly that in 2004.

Sheena King

What Will I Become?

What will I become when I let you go?
I gave birth to you
nursed you to health.
You did the same for me—
each of us growing strong
as we raised each other.

What will I become without you?
We have been together
for so many years,
the way that lovers
are together, each
dependent on/defined by
the other.

Who can I ever be without you?
When I threw back my head
unhinged my jaw,
unstuck this tongue
from the roof of my mouth
your voice would always speak,
the words brutal, keeping at bay
anyone who might hurt us—
or who might love us.

When my pen made its impression
on a piece of paper
your sonnet of molestation
would appear, unless
it was pages of haiku
recounting my fears,
a tanka, or violent villanelle
recounting our drunken stupors,
the years spent in hell.

Who will I become without you?
Our real life together was so brief,
our prison sentence too long.

You are only partly to blame, of course.
For I was afraid
of the human being I might become
if I let you go.

And so it took until today
for me to find the will I need
to let my anger go.

What will I become without you?
What will I ever be
without you?

CHAPTER 15

February 2004

Note: The names of women who participated in the House of Hope have been changed.

I had been in the aftercare support group for years. It met once a month to discuss the present. Topics varied, but they focused on our newly acquired coping skills and whether we were using them effectively in our relationships with lovers and with our families. We would discuss intimacy and affection. I was always amazed that, despite the rules forbidding it, relationships still thrived at Muncy. When I have spoken to male ex-prisoners, they've consistently told me that men don't develop personal relationships the way women inmates do. There is sex, and sometimes a close friendship. But women actively seek intimate companions in a different way, because female inmates feel such an acute need for love.

Sadly, once again, dysfunctional relationships on the inside don't differ much from dysfunctional relationships on the outside. Some are violent and abusive. Women stay in them because they are afraid to leave, terrified of being alone. Or they need someone to provide for them financially. Prison life is expensive, and wages are only pennies per hour.

On the other hand, quite a few prison relationships are loving and beautiful, and often what begins here continues and progresses on the outside after women are released—including friendships.

These were a few of our topics in the aftercare group.

When the administration decided to open the second floor of the House of Hope building, it was our support group that was given the opportunity to move there and to be housed one to a cell. I jumped at the chance, not only to live in a housing unit with other women who understood what I had been through, but also to have a cell without a cellmate.

That decision became another major turning point in my life. The newly assigned counselor and the program director wanted two people from aftercare to cofacilitate the therapeutic groups. I had already been trained to facilitate groups in the institution, and I was eager to help. I am passionate about healing from the trauma of abuse. So I was offered the position.

What began as part-time, mainly running the pre-assessment group and the evening groups for assertiveness, self-esteem, relaxation, and meditation, became a full-time job of leading the therapy sessions and conducting one-on-ones every day, all day. I would literally fall into bed at 9 p.m.—drained, emotional, and exhausted. I was wrung out, but never in my life had I felt more alive.

After a year, I was granted carte blanche. Although my methods may have been considered unorthodox at the time, the results could not be denied. Instinctively I knew what would work. I would pray first for guidance, and then I would proceed where my gut led me. In line with my training, and the traditional process at the House of Hope, I didn't force anyone to participate, but I openly shared my own experience, the person I had been, and the women I was speaking to could easily compare that to the person I had become.

In our small groups of women (affectionately dubbed "Pink Power"), we were real, raw, open, and honest. We cried together when one woman, Tammy, shared her story of being violated with a soda bottle. She was seven years old at the time. The sutures closed her wounds, but she would never bear a child.

A young, bubbly, but sarcastic and fiery twenty-two-year-old redhead named Megan told me during a one-on-one session about the prison guard she had previously had sex with and was subsequently in love with. I was bound by confidentiality and kept this information to myself, as she requested. He was much older and shared a physical likeness to the father who had molested her. In time, she saw the similarities and ended the "relationship." She was also able to deal with the hatred for her mother, who had kept her separated from her abusive father after her parents were divorced.

No charges were ever filed against him, but he was prohibited from even seeing his daughter again. In her confusion, Megan still loved her father deeply and blamed her mother for keeping the two of them separated.

Not only did we cry together, we also raged together against those who had harmed us.

There was one woman in our group, Nee, close to my own age, who never talked. I noticed that she would do the written assignments from the book we used, *The Courage to Heal*, by Ellen Bass and Laura Davis, but she would never share beyond the "feelings checklist" or the check-in that began every group. She reminded me of myself when I had been part of the inpatient groups. She was a writer. I soon learned that she was a poet.

I pondered techniques to get the quiet ones, the shy ones, the reluctant ones, like Nee, to open up. I gave an assignment to write about the one event that had the most shame attached to it and, on another page, to write down the names of those who had harmed you. When our group was assembled, two days later, in the center of our circle of chairs I placed a metal trash can. Next to this was my personal white plastic wastebasket filled with water. I saw their curious expressions as they were taking their seats. I explained that each person would read both pages, ball the papers up, and throw them into the metal trash can. When we were done, I set the papers on fire and then put the fire out with the water from my wastebasket.

Unconventional? Maybe, but when Nee read her "harmed" paper, I understood her silence and the seething rage I saw in her eyes. Every day, not only had she been molested as a child by multiple men, but her younger sister had been as well. Then, as a young adult, she was raped, and later incarcerated for trying to kill the man who had raped her five-year-old daughter.

I was irate, wanted to walk out of the room because I didn't want to lose control of myself. But I realized that my anger was justified and that justified anger is healthy, and that it is necessary for all of us to feel our anger, and express it, as an alternative to taking it out on ourselves. But now I clearly understood Nee, and slowly she began to emerge. Her poetry was painful, honest, and, in my judgment, much better than mine.

She inspired me, and in time I would call on her to assist me when I scheduled "confrontations."

The fire and water exercise, in my mind, was designed to let our past hurts burn and then drown our sorrows, thereby creating space for a rebirth. Confronting an abuser, another technique I developed, tried to reach an even deeper level. And it was a bit trickier. A group member would write a letter to her abuser and read it to my assistant, who would play the role of that abuser while I moderated the process. The goal was to release all that had been held back. Sometimes these letters would then be mailed to those who had inflicted the damage. Recently, I read in the *Philadelphia Daily News* that similar techniques are being utilized quite successfully by others today.

There were times, however, when the anger was directed at me, and then, for a brief moment at least, I would wonder if I had gone too far. I never consulted with Beth, my supervisor, before I went ahead with a new technique, because she trusted my judgment and knew my determination and commitment to helping the women heal from abuse. I did tend to worry beforehand, however, so I would always pray. But I also trust my own intuition. So whenever I was confident that the potential benefit was worth whatever risk might be involved, I would proceed without hesitation.

I knew from personal experience that it hurt to dig deep, under the Band-Aid that covered the wound. But it was necessary for healing. Treating the surface does not rid you of the infection that is affecting the course of your life when you have been violated, especially if that violation was a recurring event. It changes you. It distorts the way you see yourself and the world. Your perception has to be redefined, and the process is painful. I knew all of that, and so, after careful consideration and a review of the notes I had from several one-on-one sessions with each woman in my group, I forged ahead with a new idea.

I had been reading "The Child Within" chapter in *The Courage to Heal* when I realized that I was still confused about this subject. I had assigned the written task from the workbook and noticed that my group needed clarification, just as I did. I didn't have pictures in my possession of my nine-year-old self, and I was pretty certain that most of my group members didn't have pictures of themselves either. As an adult, it's difficult to see from a child's perspective as you wonder why it happened, why you failed to tell anyone, why your mother couldn't make him stop. It's hard to see yourself as helpless and small once you are grown. So I needed pictures.

The Parenting Department at Muncy has subscriptions to several magazines. Armed with a stack of them, and with poster boards, scissors, and tape, I went to work on a secret project. I made a collage of pictures of little girls. There were individual poster boards of magazine cutouts for each age between five and twelve.

Prior to opening the double doors of the group room before the next meeting, I stood the posters up so that they lined one wall in order by age and said a quick silent prayer. Then I yelled, "Pink Power, time for group," and stood back to watch each face as the women entered. Some were clearly surprised, others apprehensive. Two of them were angry and stomped out. No one was happy. I didn't expect anyone to be happy, but I also hadn't expected anyone to walk out.

I asked the group to be seated and look at the pictures, then turn to the "Child Within" chapter while I went to see the two who had walked out. Barbara was sitting on her bed in tears. After consoling her, I asked, "Have I ever steered you wrong?"

"No," she whispered.

"Just give it a chance."

She wiped her face, cleaned her smeared mascara and eyeliner, then marched back to the group room. I took a deep breath and went to another cell door.

"Sheena, I'm not fucking doing this!" Tracy screamed.

"You don't even know what it is," I said softly. "You just have to trust me. In order to heal, sometimes it's going to hurt, but I promise you it will not hurt for long. It's going to get better and so are you. Some things just have to be confronted if you want your life to change."

She stopped pacing back and forth in her tiny cell while swinging her arms.

She looked me in my eyes through the cell door and hissed, "I'm telling you right now—"

"Open your door."

She did and I hugged her, closed her door, and led her back to the group room with one arm around her shoulder.

I needed them to remember who they were, that they didn't cause what had happened to them, and that the little girl they had been desperately needed their love, understanding, protection, affection, and connectedness to their adult self. I didn't think this could be accomplished without a visual aid.

During the session, I asked each one to look closely at the pictures and find a little girl they identified with—one who was the age they had been when childhood was stolen from them.

"Do you see how small she is?" I asked. "Do you see the innocence in her eyes? Do you sense the love and trust she feels? Does she seem carefree and happy? She was you."

I paused, waiting for everyone to return to their seats, and asked, "How do you feel? What would you tell her?"

There were a few warnings about the people who had violated them and who they should tell about the violations, but most importantly they saw what I had hoped they would see: their own smallness, their trust, their innocence, and their helplessness. They saw that they were too young to defend themselves and that they should have been protected by someone else. They realized that they needn't be ashamed over things they hadn't caused.

After the tears were spent and I asked each of them how she felt, without exception they admitted the fear they had felt upon entering the group room that day, but they understood why I had chosen this exercise. Until that moment, they had been unable to remember how small and helpless they had been as children. It's almost impossible with your adult mind to recall how you viewed the world as a child. Tracy, who had masked her fear behind rage, said, "I don't feel like it was my fault anymore. I don't feel ashamed, like I had somehow caused it to happen to me."

Then Michele raised a question I had often asked but still couldn't answer: "I didn't even have breasts, curves, anything. What do men see in children? Why are they attracted to us?" I had a few theories, but I explained that I had never understood it either. Later, I discussed it with Beth, and she found a videotape of interviews with men who were in therapy, trying to explain what propelled them to prey on children. But this only raised more questions, deepening our anger.

The exercise had been risky, challenging, could have been psychologically damaging. But it worked.

❦

It had been hard work for all of us, and I wanted to reward them for honoring and accepting the children they had once been, so I devised a plan. But I needed permission. I asked Beth if she could arrange a few hours for my group at Project Impact for a fun day. Project Impact is a small trailer decorated like a home, a place for inmates to take children, up to age seventeen, when they come to visit. It was someplace I had enjoyed taking my own children to when they came to visit. We would sit on the small, comfortable couch and talk quietly, or at the kitchen table to draw, color, or make crafts and eat snacks. Sometimes we'd play Nintendo sitting on the beanbags in the back room, or volleyball and basketball in Impact's backyard. I figured this was the ideal place to end our lessons on the inner child.

Beth agreed and obtained administration approval. In those days, the administrative focus at Muncy was on rehabilitation and healing, not primarily on warehousing and punishment. I watched the Pink Power group of twelve survivors of sexual abuse laugh, play with toys, eat cookies, and drink Kool-Aid as they recaptured their stolen innocence. It was a beautiful moment.

Every six months, when there were graduations, I felt like one of my children was leaving home. There was pride mingled with sadness and a hope that I had truly helped them, the way I had been helped before them.

❦

There's a rule limiting how long any inmate can keep a particular job at SCI Muncy. When my time at the House of Hope was nearly done, unbeknownst to me Beth passed around a small yellow hardback journal and simply told each of the women to "just briefly write down whatever you feel." They did. I was and still am not an angel. But these kind words assured me then, and continue to assure me today, that I had done what I had set out to do: I had helped them. In the midst of my own nightmare, I had been able to live this dream.

I will never forget any of these women, because it was the first time I really felt as if I had made a positive difference in someone else's life. Many people told me that I saved their lives, but really we saved each other. I had finally conquered my fear—a hidden and up-to-then-unnamed fear—of being useless and irrelevant.

Nee Sims

Outside Observer

(No one dared to uncover the secrets she buried well...
It seems almost hidden, that pain beneath the shell...)

My spirit had been deeply damaged by the roving eyes and hands of men and females who ripped my innocence to a thousand pieces. My outside shell covered deeply rooted feelings of self-hatred, shame, confusion and emptiness... I would have given anything to be able to run away from the person inside me so I could escape somehow, but I was stuck with "me"—a person I didn't truly care for. I stood looking at her as an outside observer...

She disconnects to protect the fragile child inside.
She swings the gate to the hands of hate
    and freely gives her prize.
Sex is nothing but holes and humping, the body's need for release.
But when his dick slides in she's sick within and her mind
    is never free.

She blocks him out; her insides shout but there's calm
written on her face.
I see her die; I hear her cry but the tears must have been erased.
Whoever had a notion that sex meant emotion
forgot to let her know.
She's enthused while she's being used and self-hate
begins to grow.
He has his fun and until he's done, her soul has turned jet black.
She disappears while he's in there and I won't let her come back.
Why does she cringe so much? She hates the touch
and she could never escape.
She shuts her feelings off to become the boss
and takes control before it's too late.
It's always the same how she plays the game;
I stand up and applaud her.
I observe from outside ... the woman's still alive and
I thank God I'm not her.

Entries from Beth's Yellow Journal

Sheena—you are a very special woman with a very special gift. Thank you for being a valuable peer facilitator; you have made my job a lot easier and I enjoy working with you and your fresh ideas. More changes are on the way and I truly appreciate your enthusiasm. God Bless—Beth

Sheena, you made facing my fears seem like the easiest thing in the world to do and it was a pleasure having you as my group facilitator. I never knew you could make so many thugs cry at once ☺. Thanks for all you did and all you will continue to do for me as I battle my issues. Much love—Sharon

Sheena, you are more than just another peer to me. You are a blessing from God who inspires others. You have a way with words that captures others and makes them listen. You're special to me and I pray that God will show mercy and grace with you so you can reunite with your friends and family at home. —Dot

You already know how much you mean to me. There are no more words to describe it. I will never forget the impact you had on my life. I am truly a better person and it gets better every day. The pink group will never be the same if they make you move on, but for me, Pink Power forever. Thank you for making me feel a part of something so important. I love you sista for life. Always—Wanda

Sheena, Hey Sunshine! I know I told you a number of times how much you've touched my life, and how very special you are to me, but there are no words to express this strongly enough. You will always be in my heart, and your gifts to me always a part of my new life. You are truly a blessing to so many. Love—Rita

My hero, my mentor, my inspiration. There are no words to describe the admiration and depth of gratitude I feel for you. Thanks for your compassion, your honesty, and your persistence in helping me on the journey to become a survivor, and no longer a victim. I've always looked up to you. And having you share your pain and experience just allowed my respect and awe to grow. You're a beautiful, talented, and gifted woman and I'm so glad that our paths have crossed. Every one of us is blessed to have known you. Thank you just for being you. Everything you do is for the greater good, and it's nice to be understood. —Chanté

Sheena, I'll keep this short—so I won't get too "mushy." You are more to me than I can find the words for. I look up to you in many ways and the love I have and feel for you is pure and unconditional. I look forward to the work I have to do because I know you will be there to help me along. You've been blessed with a gift and I'm so glad I'm getting some of it. You're so beautiful Sheena and I wish nothing but the best for you. Love Ya—Malia

I'm very appreciative of you and the work you do. I think that with all the trials you've been through you are a wonderful person because of them. You let me see that this ain't the end of the road and I am inspired. I will never forget you, nor do I want to. —Benai

First let me say I love you very much from the day I met you, and now today, this year, this minute. I have grown so close to you. I feel like I know you more and I know there won't be no other year that someone like you will come my way. God bless you always. Te amo mi amiga. —Maria

My dearest friend, I could go on and on to express what a gift you have been in my life. You helped me to believe in me and always, always know exactly what to say when I'm going through a crisis. You are not just a gift to me; you are a gift to anyone who is lucky enough to cross your path. You are a gifted, beautiful woman and the group will never be the same. I love you my friend, my mentor too. —Karen

Dear Sheena, I want you to know that you've made a major impact in my life. You've bandaged a broken spirit I never thought I could recover from and enlightened me in ways that I never imagined possible. I'm so blessed that God placed you in my life. To you I will be forever grateful. Love always—Nicky

Sheena—What can I say ... but thank you from the bottom of my heart. And I stand on our Father's promise: "He that has begun a good work in me (us) will continue it, until the day of Christ Jesus." I've just started on another journey. The road we endured together, finding me, was made possible by YOU! Thank you again. Love—Carol

Sheena ≈≈≈♥, You possess so many great qualities that I deeply admire. I look up to you so much. You are so strong and driven. You know who you are and you hold your head high. I am so blessed to have met you and to have you as my peer facilitator. We (the whole group) are blessed. You have a calling from God. I wish I had more time with you to learn, but what I did learn I will carry with me. I will never forget you. You are an angel. Love—Jenny

Sheena King

Senryu

Walk in to the wind.
Hold head high, shoulders squared
in search of self love

CHAPTER 16

March 2012

I waited for the doctor to give me the results of yet another biopsy on my cervix. He thought it was scar tissue. I hoped it was, but he wanted to be certain. Did I mention that like Jay-Z, "I hate waiting"? The longer I waited, the more I worried; the more I worried, the more I twisted my hair.

Conscious of my appearance, I tried to stop the twisting and worrying, so I prayed, "Please, please God, don't let it be anything more than scar tissue. Please. I promise I'll be good. I'll go back to church."

I had to smile to myself, despite the fear, when I realized I was bargaining with God—much the way I did as a five-year-old when my mother stomped me. Not long after that incident, I stopped praying to God. I stopped believing in God. My rationale was: *There can't be a God who would allow these things to happen to me. If there was a God, why didn't He stop me from being hurt? Where is He?*

So I didn't believe until I did the unthinkable by committing a major crime and then found myself on my knees begging God to forgive me and not spare my life. A strange thing happened, which I have already described to you: Little by little, God showed me He was real. I thought about that journey when my gynecologist confirmed what he thought it was: scar tissue. I left his exam room thanking God again.

In the mail that night, I found an invitation to speak to women who were recovering from drug and alcohol addictions. The topic was the trauma of abuse.

I looked around at the faces of so many women, ranging in age from early twenties to late forties. Their eyes were expectant—some showing skepticism, while others were downcast as if to hide their shame. I felt overwhelmed with sadness and apprehension. *What am I supposed to say to these women to make a difference? How can I help anyone when I can barely help myself?*

I said a silent prayer to the God I hadn't believed in until my life experiences showed me that He was and is real. Then I sat down among the women. I didn't want to stand over them, because I wanted them to understand that I wasn't better or above anyone else. I was one with them. I was not only a survivor of sexual abuse and domestic violence, I was also a convicted felon. I whispered one of my favorite verses: "I can do all things through Christ who strengthens me." Then I opened my mouth to speak. I don't know what I said, but I could hear the raw emotion in my voice as I shared my journey with them. To close, I read four entries from my journal—which I also share with you, scattered on different pages of this book.

When I finished, there wasn't a dry eye and the applause was deafening. It was also uncomfortable. I was unprepared for what happened next. Many of the women began to share their stories of pain, of abuse, of the shame and guilt that attaches itself and doesn't let go. In that moment, I knew that true healing was possible, but I couldn't do it alone. And I could help them as I continued to heal myself. Healing from abuse doesn't go in a straight line. You take one step forward by learning something new about yourself, like realizing and accepting that it wasn't your fault, then you take two steps backward by finding yourself in yet another abusive relationship. I had taken entire city-size blocks backward! Before I sat down among my peers, I didn't think I had anything to offer them except similar experiences and a heart filled with compassion. I found out that these things were all I needed—along with a lot of prayer.

Not one of the women who shared themselves so completely, who trusted in my healing process and did the work on themselves (despite the crippling pain) to truly heal from sexual abuse, has ever returned to this prison. Being a part of that process was the greatest compensation I could have had. I don't crave the spotlight. I simply need to make a difference. I have only limited opportunities to atone or make amends, but I will always do what I can if I am able to help someone else. I made that promise to myself and to my children, and I cannot break a promise to them, just as I cannot forget their soft brown eyes spilling tears down cherubic cheeks.

That image breaks my heart a little more each time I recall it. "But Mom, why can't you come home with us?"

Keeva was nine and Keiff was six. I was out of breath because my son had created an obstacle course in the visiting room's play area. With the honest innocence of a child, he told me, "Mommy, you're getting fat." His solution was to exercise me.

I held them close to me, kissed their tears, and told them the truth about my life. They were too young for all the details, but they are my children and I swore to never lie to them. They are also inner-city kids, and even in their innocence they were still wise to the dangers of the street and the ways of the world.

"When you are bad, there are consequences. But I promise I've made myself better, and for all the bad I've done to people, I will do better."

I don't regret my honest communication with my children, because it made our relationship stronger. The bond we have with each other is unbreakable. That was the first visit we had that didn't end in tears. The end of every visit with my family, particularly my children, is excruciatingly painful.

There are no words to describe it. After twenty-two years it's still not easy, but we've adapted, because I remind myself that it's a blessing simply to be afforded the opportunity to spend time with my children. So many parents don't. There is one woman in particular who didn't see her children become adults because of my actions, and that realization dries my selfish tears immediately. How can I cry when, despite the physical separation, I was still able to be fully involved in raising my children through mail, phone calls, and occasional visits? I was in contact with their teachers and received reports from the case workers who led their group therapy—assisting children with an incarcerated parent to cope—through the Philadelphia Society for Services for Children. How can I complain? How can I cry?

I cried anyway, because what the head knows, the heart may not readily accept. Just as my son knew that I had a life sentence for a crime I had committed, his heart couldn't accept that in Pennsylvania "life" means exactly that.

There was one visit that I will never forget. If old age brings dementia or Alzheimer's, this visit will probably still remain the most lucid memory I have. The visiting room was packed, as it normally is when there's a bus trip from Philadelphia, especially when the Kids 'n' Kin program was able to provide bimonthly visits for free for women with children. While my children were arguing over what to choose from the vending machines, I let my eyes and mind roam around the visiting room. I smiled at young mothers holding babies who slept contentedly in their arms. I fought back my own tears when children cried and held tightly to their mothers as their visits ended and their mothers' tears flowed freely. I eavesdropped on heated discussions over money or infidelity between partners, and laughed at small children playing with toys or running carefree around the visiting room until the officer called the inmates to the desk, admonishing them to get their children "under control" or their visit would be "terminated."

I was sitting with my own mother. "Mom, these officers are ridiculous," I whispered in anger. "They're just children doing what children do!"

"Sheena, relax your eyebrows. I need to tell you about your son before they come back. Your son, our boy, is mad at the world. He's fighting, getting into trouble in school. He punched somebody in the face because she was teasing him about you being in jail."

It's amazing—your heart can break so many times and, somehow, it still beats.

After we shared a few sandwiches, wing dings, chips, and butterscotch Krimpets, along with some orange and apple juice, I took my children to the Project Impact trailer. While my daughter entertained herself with crafts, I went to shoot some hoops with my son. He was always a gifted athlete. Breathless and sweating profusely, I leaned against the gate and called Keiff to me. He continued to dribble the ball as I coaxed him into telling me about his feelings.

I could sense the anger rolling through him like waves, just as I could feel the summer heat cooking my skin through the visiting room jumpsuit. I watched his eyebrows knit together on a face identical to my own and braced myself for what was to come. He exploded: "I'm mad because my friends invite me to their houses to meet their moms and I can't do that! Why was you stupid? You're stupid!"

It was hard to breathe with a lump in my throat. I held him to me.

"Keiff, I'm so sorry. I'm so, so sorry. If I could change anything, I would change everything except having you and Keeva. I'm so sorry."

After a moment, I felt his body relax, and he hugged me back, never releasing the basketball from his large right hand. I kissed his head before he pulled away to make a perfect half-court shot. Then I regained my composure and fought back my tears by reminding myself that this wasn't about me. It was for and about him. He needed to be able to express himself without fear of punishment. It was better for him to say what he felt instead of acting out.

While he made foul shots and layups, we discussed appropriate ways of expressing emotions and why he should not hit a girl. He seemed to understand after I asked him how he would feel if a man hit me or a boy hit his sister. The anger appeared again, but he acknowledged and accepted my point.

In the privacy of my cell that night, I cried audibly like a wounded animal. In a sense, I was a wounded animal. The honesty of my son's words and the pain he felt because of my actions had wounded me. I reflected on his anger and was dismayed to realize that it mirrored my own. If I wanted him to work on finding positive outlets for his volatile emotions, then I had to do the same. I had vowed that I wouldn't be the type of mother who said, "Do as

I say, not as I do," the way my own mother had. I needed to make additional changes in order to set an example for him.

It was at this moment that I flashed backward through my angry outbursts, remembering the time I threw a chair when too many people were standing in front of the shower I was trying to exit. I saw my eye blackened and sealed shut from the fist of a girl I loved after I pushed her down the steps in a fit of jealousy. I heard a friend tell me, with tears in her eyes, "Sheena, you have to control your anger! I had a dream that you were sent to the hole for fighting."

My mind wandered further backward, until I saw my mother through my own five-year-old eyes. She had cut her long hair to a very short cap of black curls. The kids on my block teased me: "Your mom looks like a boy." I hit one girl repeatedly. I could find a hundred reasons to justify my anger.

But they would simply have been excuses. When you know better, you do better. I know that I was born into violence inflicted by angry parents. I know that I am emotional and my temper is quick. I know that I can close my eyes and see hands slapping and punching me. I can also see my hands strike back.

I carried my son in a body filled with anger, fear, paranoia. My mother had previously carried me while feeling the same emotions. This cycle, just like the cycle of molestation in my family, would have to end. I can't stop the varied forms of cancer that have ravaged my family members, but I can control my reaction to situations and teach my son to do the same. It's been difficult for both of us to change and become better people, but the benefits make it worth the struggle.

The life I took away can never be brought back. This is a truth I live with daily as a far greater punishment than the prison sentence I'm presently serving. But there are other things I have ruined that can be rehabilitated, and so I'm determined to restore as much as I possibly can in the time I have left on this earth.

❦

Sheena King

Where Do I Fit?

I am alone in this world
filled with people
feigning affection,

love,
innocence.

Those who pretend to feel me,
understand me,
are they sincere in their friendship?
And what of the "me" no one knows?

Yet they judge.
They whisper on street corners,
in their quiet places
where they meet by twos
by threes
by fours.

Oh how they love each other,
or so they say.
Why is this so seldom on display?

I examine and analyze these things
from above,
from beneath
never from beside.

I don't fit
I am not cliqued or clichéd.
I stand alone,

the way truth stands alone,
always true
to itself,
to myself.

Journal Entry: August 11, 1998

My mom told me something that rocked my world. What she told me will take our relationship to another level. Getting secrets out really does help. I asked her if what had happened to me ever happened to her. I couldn't come out and just ask her if she'd ever been molested, because I still feel like a kid when it's time to talk to her. She told me that a cousin, another cousin, an uncle, and a friend of the family had molested her. She said the first time it happened she was only three! I forgot all about myself because I was so outraged that someone dared to touch my mother.

We held each other and cried. I'm just so shocked that it didn't turn out the way I thought it would, with much screaming and accusations like it always has in the past. She'd yell and I'd submit, be meek and quiet, and agree to everything she said. This was different. It was scary, but touching. I should have known, from her accusations when she caught Jeff that one time, that something had happened to her and no one did anything to protect her or save her. I wish I had known then what I know now. Our relationship could have been different. My life could have been different.

The two passages by Nadine Nicholson and Wyanda Holman below were composed in response to a group writing prompt: to "write about the first time you told or talked about the violations you were forced to endure."

Writing Exercise: Nadine Nicholson

Grandpa comes and takes Aunt Althea and me to McDonald's to eat French fries. I can play there and eat nuggets. Sometimes

Mommy comes and feeds me nuggets. Then we go to Grandma's house and I get in the bath and brush my teeth. I get in the bed, but I don't sleep. Grandma falls asleep with the TV on so I watch it while she is sleeping. It feels so good to be young and get love.

Everything has changed, something is wrong. Mommy hits me. I don't know why. All I know is Grandma has to take me to the hospital. I don't like Mommy mad at me. I love Mommy, don't she love me?

Aunt Althea has a new boyfriend; his name is Frank. I like Frank. He picks me up with his arms because he is big and strong. Is this how my daddy would be? Where is my daddy at? Maybe Frank can be my daddy. Maybe I can call him daddy.

The years passed with Uncle Frank touching and feeling me whenever he could. You are so pretty, he would say. You smell good. I hated him around but I was used to it. I was eighteen years old when I first told on my uncle. It was an accident when I told. My aunt accused me of stealing her bracelet. When I tried to explain myself to her, she called me a thief, and a liar. I got so mad that she would not listen to me that I screamed out, "Tell your husband to keep his hands off me!"

My aunt told me I was a lying whore and a bitch. Why should she believe me?

All these years of it and I never said a word. I never spoke the words, "He did this to me." My telling came out in different ways. I did everything from set fires, lie, and steal, run away, to having consensual sex. My aunt was right, who would believe a lying, stealing whore like me.

I sit in this class, in this prison; I cry for the people I have hurt along the way. It is here that I have grown. I know that I cannot do this alone. I consider myself lucky to be alive, to live to remember. There are other girls like me here—we are not alone.

Writing Exercise: Wyanda Holman

Growing up being a victim of child abuse has been very rough for me. I had been abused at the age of seven and numerous times after. While little girls were wandering around playing with Barbie or riding bikes or even watching their favorite television shows, I, on the other hand, was dealing with so many emotions from being molested.

Throughout my life, I continuously replayed my abuser pumping my lifeless body. In those times, I would become very angry toward myself—more than others. I was confused and had a load of unanswered questions. I wanted to know why I had to be the one he chose to hurt. What kind of person does something that perverse to a child?

He lived out his sick fantasies on me! My pain inflicted deep emotional scars that I chose to suppress for many years. One thing about sickness—if you don't treat it properly, it will spread. From the age of seven through twenty-seven, I started my journey on a very wide path of destruction.

The layers of my life consisted of lies, sex, drugs, and most of all hatred. I had the emptiness within that I tried to fulfill with sex. I controlled every relationship using sex as a weapon and hatred for the opposite sex as a shield—never realizing that while I inflicted hurt on others, I was actually devaluing my own self-worth.

For many years, I believed that in order to make a man content, give him good sex. I am very proud to say that my self-esteem isn't as low now. I started therapeutic treatment and became aware of my self-destructive patterns. I thank God for giving me the courage to open up and talk about the sexual abuse and how it honestly affected my life. Through therapy, I finally allowed myself to actually feel again, and I eventually replaced that self-hatred with self-fulfilling love.

Sharing with other women who have suffered the same pain, I have realized that I wasn't alone in rebuilding my life. We form a sisterhood through our rebirth, using our groups as new awakenings. We collectively draw from each other's strengths as well as weaknesses in order to rebuild our courage, to take steps toward healing and survivorship.

Nee Sims

Baby Girl Who Knows So Little

It's a pity to see the innocence of you upon a podium,
being free in your carelessness ... Eyes wide
and heart unshielded ...
You are searching for that great unknown, delivering
your innocence into the arms, the trust, the care of ... those—
those who take you for granted.

Your fragile sensibilities can't understand why you feel alone
in a crowded room, or why your heart aches beyond reason ...
why your gift is always left unopened when they
    caress the ribbons
that surround the package of you.

Baby girl, you know so little ...
You know nothing of the patience that must be harnessed
in slowly discovering your hidden beauties, and nothing
of the kiss that hopes to reach your soul,

rather than be a prelude to simple
desires ...

My child, you can't discern the difference between the touch
that's meant to comfort you and accept you ...
and the one that wants to arouse your passions
so they can fulfill their physical yearnings.

I want so bad to teach you what a precious thing it is to love
and be loved ... but my own young heart
knows the sad reality ... the reality
that you're not gonna understand it overnight,
that you won't find its meaning
by some other person's guidelines ...
I wish that I could teach you how uniquely fulfilling it is

to realize that love is so much more than physical;
it's a passion of a different kind.

It hurts me to see your young and innocent heart so deceived, so
devalued and misunderstood ... but there is nothing
I can teach you today
that will protect you from tomorrow...

My baby, you know so little!

Postscript

Writing was and still is essential for my healing process, and it has also proved productive for many of the women I have been honored to sit in a circle with at various times. Rereading their poems and a few from my book as I prepare this manuscript reminds me of the figurative slap I received when my book of poems was published.

"Mom-Mom, some of my poems were published in a book!"

"That's great, Nay."

I looked at my aunt. "Auntie, not like they were before when a poem was published in a newspaper or a few anthologies. No, these are all my poems with a picture of me on the back of the book."

"Nay-Nay, I'm so proud of you."

Nevertheless, when they read the synopsis of the book from the promotional flyer, the opinions of my family changed. They saw words like "incest," "rape," and "molestation."

"Why would you do that?" my aunt queried.

"It's like pouring salt on an old wound," Mom-Mom said.

What?

"Why are you bringing back old stuff?"

Huh?

"Let sleeping dogs lie!"

Seriously?

They clichéd me to death. I couldn't believe what I was hearing. My family, the people I loved the most in this world, wouldn't read my book.

My view was one-sided, so my feelings were hurt. It took my then-sixteen-year-old daughter to broaden my perspective: "Mom,

Grandmom said your poems got published in a book. What's it called?"

"*UnHeard Soul*."

"I want to read it."

"Are you sure?"

"Yeah."

"Well, no one at home has a copy, because no one wants to read it, so I'll have to send you a copy," I said, pouting.

I could hear the disappointment in my voice. My children and I are attuned to one another. We easily notice each other's moods and emotions.

"Mom, I heard the family talking and everyone is proud of you, but they don't know how to deal with what happened to you, so they don't really want to be reminded."

Oh.

She continued, "But Mom, you already told me and Keiff about the things that happened, so I want to read it."

I sent her a copy of the book.

"Mom, when I read your poems, I felt so sad. They made me cry. Your oldest niece read the book too."

My niece—wow!

"That's not all—Grandma read the book too."

"Did she? That's surprising. What did she say?"

"Well, she actually read it before I did and she was crying, saying, 'She hates me. Sheena hates me.'"

That broke my heart, because it wasn't my intention. I don't hate my mother. I felt misunderstood.

This reminded me of a previous interview about a few of my published poems. One of the questions I was asked was why I write. I write for the same reason that I breathe. I don't know how not to. It's natural for me and easier than talking. I explained to my daughter that writing poetry and prose is therapeutic for me. It's a constructive way for me to express my anguish and emotions. It enables me to see what's really going on within me, instead of keeping it inside, pretending that I'm fine, and allowing things to fester and build until I explode. I wish I would have practiced it as an outlet before I ruined so many lives.

My daughter listened carefully before she said, "I told Grandma that you don't hate her, but when she cried, I started crying, then my brother and my cousins cried too."

I felt horrible. "Kee, I wanted the book to be published because it was a huge part of my healing process. When you keep these things a secret, you allow it to happen to someone else, especially with incest. Maybe if I had told someone who would listen, I could have kept it from happening to my sister.

"Look at our family, Kee. The same things that happened to me happened to your aunt, but we each handled it differently. I took my anger out on others, but she took it out on herself. In prison, I had inpatient therapy, but she didn't receive help, so her mind turned on itself and she developed schizophrenia."

"But why does Grandma think you hate her?"

"Probably because she blames herself and feels guilty. Kee, I don't want her to hurt, but I make no apology for my own healing process, and if my poems help someone else then that's even better." My daughter smiled, grabbed my hand, and deftly changed the subject.

Later that night, I thought about my mom crying and saying that I hated her. Hurt by her, yes, but hatred now? No. In order for me to move forward for myself, I had to forgive her and others too—not for them, but for me. I also had to forgive them for my children.

As long as I harbored anger, hatred, fear, and resentment in my heart, I would have a stranglehold on my children. That stranglehold had a negative effect on my relationship with them. Therefore, I forgave my mom.

I also forgave Daymond, because my son loved him and had seen a side of him that I hadn't seen. I saw the crack addict who brought grief and pain to my mother, my sisters, and me. My son, Keiff, saw the recovered addict that he called Pop-Pop.

I also forgave because I didn't want the darkness that I held on to inside of me to kill me.

I called my mom to comfort her, but she surprised me. "Sheena, I'm sorry. You're not even here and you're a better mother to your children than I was."

She was crying and I knew she was sincere. My entire childhood I had longed for her apology and recognition. I had imagined that I would gloat and smile knowingly like the Cheshire Cat. Instead, I felt nothing except amazed that she could acknowledge how I tried hard to be the best mother I could be, even from a great distance.

Early the next morning, I spread my photo albums out on the bed with me, trying not to feel the familiar pain of watching my children grow through the eye of cameras. I stared at the pictures of my two children, my nieces, my nephews. Although I hated what had happened to me, my soul was at peace, because the children in my family were safe. Exposing what had happened to me and having the courage to stop biting my tongue and a willingness to reveal my reality had saved these children from experiencing the horror that I had lived through. And my willingness to be honest about my life has, I know, helped many others through the difficult process of putting the pieces together after sexual abuse, incest, rape, and molestation. Instead of crying as I normally do when faced with the fact that my children grew up physically separated from me, I smiled at their smiling faces. Yes, in many ways, I've ruined my life and the lives of others, but maybe my story will change someone else's life. If it does, then everything I've endured was worth it.

I could say that my parents destroyed me, my community disregarded me, and the system failed me. It would all be true. However, if I took that road, then when would I accept responsibility for the choices I've made, and how? I failed myself. I didn't believe in myself, nor did I fight hard enough to make something of the hand I had been dealt. I couldn't change my past. I still can't, but I can change my present. I see this as my beginning.

EPILOGUE

I Chose Love

Love was an emotion that I had been denied—because it was inadequately displayed by my mother, and perversely given by my father and stepfather. While I was in therapy, I chose love.

Loving myself was crucial if I was ever to learn how to love someone else. It took a few years for me to realize that I could love someone romantically and intimately. It took a little longer for me to learn that I actually deserved to be loved totally, completely, and unconditionally. Even after therapy, I suffered from low self-esteem, and if you don't feel yourself worthy of love, you won't receive it—or, if you do, you won't believe it, so you'll push the other person away. Luckily for me, I found someone who loved me enough to push back. She had also benefited from therapy and fully understood what I was going through.

In addition, I needed to educate myself about how to love my children the right way while showing them, too, how to love, how to be affectionate, how to accept their own value and develop a sense of self-worth. I won't say that all my relationships with subsequent lovers, or with Keeva and Keiff, have been perfect. Most of them weren't even close. I've shed many, many tears, cried out to God, and even believed at times that I must have been meant to be alone. Still, I kept myself open to being in love, since I enjoyed the feeling of having been loved. I found that I needed someone to share and to build with, so I tried it again.

If we are lucky, with age comes experience and wisdom—and we learn the differences between expressions of love. Passionate love is a "wildly emotional state in which tender and sexual feelings, elation and pain, anxiety and relief, altruism and jealousy coexist in a confusion of feelings," according to social psychologists

Ellen Berscheid and Elaine Walster. That was the love I sought, but it's a state that can't be sustained for long, so it quickly faded or caused me to desperately hold on too tightly. And when you hold someone too tightly, you kill them. It's a hard lesson to learn, but a valuable one. I eventually realized that passionate love will not grow or evolve as companionate love does. This second kind of love is what marriages that last decades are made from.

After years of being denied love, being confused about it, having my heart shattered, giving it up, then yearning for it again, I finally have it. Relationships aren't perfect, because people aren't perfect, just like families aren't. However, real love is perfection, and I found the perfect one for me. I know I deserve it ... and so do you.

I read the following thought somewhere, I can't remember where, and it had a profound effect on me: There comes a point in your life when you realize who matters, who never did, who won't anymore ... and who always will. So don't worry about people from your past. There's a reason they didn't make it to your future.

And in this way I found my future.

All of this is reflected in the poetry I composed while in the process of recovery and personal rediscovery. Some of these poems I have already shared. I include a few more in conclusion.

Until You

Taste buds never differentiated salt or sweet until
I tasted you.
I couldn't talk until you touched my lips and
bid me speak.
I wouldn't walk until you
held my hand.
I was blind until you
opened my eyes.
There was no hearing until you
whispered my name.
I wasn't breathing until you
breathed into me.
I wasn't dreaming until you
rocked me to sleep.

I Found

I have found the perfect woman, professing to never forsake me.
If you are a figment or dream—don't ever wake me.
There's still, you see a little girl inside who believes in fairy tales:
ever-searching for happy endings, big pots of gold, gentle males.
She endured the Boogey-Man, fled monsters under her bed—
no real males, conniving men, preying upon children too easily led!
Like the maiden in distress, waiting for the knight who never came,
she had a life of total madness, absorbed the faults,
the hurt, the shame.
So if her dreaming brings her rapture and other wonders
absent in the past,

then let me sleep this sleep of blissful peace
and make this dream my last.

Dead Ash

Such sadness fills my quiet heart with pain.
You do not love me, I've known this quite some time.
Your vacant eyes, to me, are not the same:
Our conversations are now pantomimed.
Piles of gray ash sit in the fireplace,
No fragrant scent of mirth, just fetid air,
Harsh silence in this overcrowded space.
Living alone will be my greatest fear—
Wasted years are fading memories
Of my adhesion to a union code,
And that which I have dreamed—of what we couldn't be—
with eyes too blind this marriage did corrode.
Behind me, nights of torment as I cry.
With bags in tow, I'll gladly say "goodbye."

Untitled No. 2

As a moth to the flame
your heat draws me.
I attempt avoidance; to ignore you
or pretend I don't feel
the gravity of your gaze.
It ignites my fire.
When you call my name
my heart pounds.
Smooth skin roughens.
You walk too close.
I feign innocence,
request the circle of your arms
to soothe me, ease me, cool me.
I want to burn.

Tanka Sequence

O' how I long
to shed this dreadful skin
to be rid of
the sagging dimpled sinful
flesh of lust

Unzip me
with tenderness and caution
zip me down
reveal the bones this skin holds
the heart that beats for no one

Take this heart of mine
alter the rhythmic beating
to beat for life
to beat for love everlasting
to beat until our souls dance

Intersection

Our lines intersect.
They've crossed each other and blurred
into one continuous string. I
no longer know where you end
and I begin.
where I end
and you begin.

So I hang tenaciously to this thread,
suspended by fear that it will snap
as the hurricane of our love
blows it fro and to.

Am I still an independent soul
if my loop is linked to yours?
if I've encouraged you to knot it
and keep me captive—
safe from myself?
Have I lost the me that I became?
Do I snap this string,
yank me inside myself
before I lose myself,
and allow you to break the me
that I've built, destroyed, and recreated
into an I before we meshed
and I became your Mrs.?

Untitled No. 3

I could confide,
never had to hide
behind the lies.
I was truth.
I was trust.
I was for us.
Yet you dared not give enough.
You were deceit.
Clichés of/friends to the end of…
What?
Where's the proof?
Devoted and real.
Loyalty one might feel.
My heart that will not heal
is not defeat.

Learning from pain,
sagacity for the brain.
Rainbows after the rain?

Untitled No. 4

There was a hole in my heart you carefully healed.
An empty void inside you patiently filled.
Permanent fixture—a smile on my face.
The sound of my laughter boomed through space.
A twinkle in my eye, replaced the tears.
The strength of your presence alleviates my fears.
No more sleepless nights
holding a pillow tightly in my bed.
We'd grow old together, that's what you said.
But you grew young while I grew old,
my love for you blossomed while yours turned cold.
What you once nourished, now you bleed dry.
The mythical vampire…
I'm quite dead inside.

A Fat Girl's Substitute

You were my passion
my addiction
You were my compulsion
my obsession
Now you are gone.
Food is my constant
companion.

Breathe

I need this
space
between us to
decrease
until we are
breathing
the same air,
until my
inhale
is your
exhale.

’Til then,
I’ll hold
my breath.

Come back to me.

Untitled No. 5

When we walk,
we are in step.
When we talk
we are in tune.
When I'm lost
in your eyes
I'm in touch
with your soul.
Our lives are
twined.
Our hearts are
infused.
We are in
to each other,
in love.

Newlywed

Will it always be this way?
I lay awake last night to watch
you sleep. I was so overwhelmed
that dreams eluded me.

Will it always be this way?
Your fingertips left singed
marks on my flesh, while
your searching lips found
places I never knew were there.

Will it always be this way?
Our bodies meet, merge,
bring pleasures my mind
doesn't comprehend. After
hours of exploring paradise,
we stop to begin again.

Will it always be this way?
I awaken to the feeling
of your arms around me.
We lie here like two spoons,
made from the same mold,
made for each other's form.
We hold tightly, as if
to never let go, as if
our lives depended
on the holding.

Will it always be this way?
Kaya Shapiro

When you touch me, I am alive, I am beautiful. I am whole.
My constant partner. In your hands there is strength, desire,

expertise. My infinite lover.
When I'm in your arms, I feel admired.
I feel secure. My forever refuge.
In your eyes, there is compassion,
my future, my soul. My eternal companion.

When I brought to you
the broken pieces of my heart,
the chaotic confusion of my life,
the borderlines of my personality,
you healed me. In the comfort of your love
and the peace of your presence
you touched me with your eyes, your hands, your heart.
And I am forever changed. You are the half to my whole,
the better part of my soul.

We Shall Share

There shall be no labor that we do not share in
to strengthen, motivate, uplift, and encourage.

There shall be no sorrow that we
won't endure together.

We shall share in the joys of this existence
and minister to each other through all pain.

For there is no greater love than this:
a love shared by two souls, joined for life.

Breathe 'til Breath

I love you until I breathe my last breath,
'til there's only you and none of me left.
'Til I am a pile of bones, teeth, and hair,
a splatter of matter of wretched years:
of wordless pleading with air in my lungs
wanting to exhale 'til unconsciousness comes.
Of futile searches for reasons to breathe,
paradoxical hopes for swift reprieves,
then you surged inside as a cleansing breath
implosions of love—there's none of me left.

I Owe You

The search is over, pure love long last.
The slate has been cleared; I've forgotten my past.
I sought understanding, acknowledgment of worth,
to be treated like a lady—preferably first.

You've given me these things and so much more
of which I hadn't dreamt or thought before:
A love with gentleness,
my muse of intrigue, no sign of ennui.

You entered my life, not by chance
but by God's choosing, part of His plan,
designed and crafted by His perfect will.
Each empty place you perfectly filled.
The beat of my heart, its rhythmic flow for you,
is the motivating force I now owe my life to.

You search me. You see me. You know me—
everything about me: my vulnerability, my
shame in those things I dare not name.
My soul I've bared before your searching eye.
Silently you witnessed the dark places
I've journeyed through but stayed too long.
The wrongs I've done to those I've harmed.
The evil of a heart blackened and
calloused by pain. You've observed
the indulgence of my flesh, and wept.

Your eyes widened when I was invaded by
a light that penetrated my soul and scorched
the crust from my heart. You grin at the love
I've shared, the faith I've shown.

You search me, you see me, you know me
everything about me.
Yet, still I am your "Great One."

Afterword

The healing journey was not a linear one for me. There were starts and stops, forward motion and backpedaling to those old, comfortable, and unhealthy ways of coping through flashbacks and retraumatization. I would love to say that once the healing process begins, life gets easier. It does not, at least not for me, but things did begin to make sense about myself. For much of my youth, I viewed myself as a monster or a deviant because of the choices I had made, especially leading to my incarceration.

Submerged introduced me to people I likely would not have met. People who saw more in me than I had yet to see in myself. People who helped me to stretch beyond my self-erected barricades. People who believe in me and strongly believe that I deserve a second chance at freedom, because they recognize that I have never truly been free. They saw redeeming, transformative qualities, very real change, and my continuing desire to heal and grow into a much better version of myself. People like Bret Grote and his team, Steve Bloom, Vikki Law, Valerie Kiebala, and so many others.

Because of them, *Submerged* has progressed from a self-published book to gaining the interest of PM Press. As I began to fully believe in myself, I prayed that a publisher would take a chance on this book, and I am thankful for alignment, because

Submerged would not have reached your hands without them, and I am so grateful that it did.

Submerged also led other incarcerated women to me who have endured similar experiences, and although I no longer work in the House of Hope, I am able to continue living out my passion of helping others heal, through one-on-one counseling as a certified peer support specialist and Christian counselor, leading a Bible study in my housing unit as I pursue a master's degree in Pastoral Ministry, and passing around the dog-eared copy of my story.

I have also been invited to speak about my total healing journey and transcendence above my circumstances at a graduation for long-term offenders and to the women in the alcohol and other drugs (AOD) therapeutic community. These are humbling experiences that would not have occurred had I not had the courage to push beyond the secrets that held me captive and expose it all in the pages of *Submerged.*

I will, therefore, repeat what I wrote in the introduction to this book almost a decade ago: Tell your story to heal yourself and to heal someone else. You have no idea whose life you might touch or who you could help save until you do.

Sheena Monique King
January 2024

Editor's Note

Steve Bloom

September 2014—I first met Sheena King in April of this year. I might have met her a month earlier, in March, the first time I visited the prison where she resides: SCI (State Correctional Institution) Muncy, named for its proximity to Muncy, Pennsylvania—a small town set in rolling countryside of farmland and other small towns just south of the more mountainous terrain for which central Pennsylvania is rightly famous. It would be a nice part of the world to live in, if you didn't live in a prison.

Why my meeting with Sheena was delayed until my second visit is not particularly important. It was one of those things that happen because of the arbitrary ways in which prisons work. What is important, however, is why I decided to visit SCI Muncy in the first place, so I will take a moment to share that story with you.

I had seen poems by several women who were incarcerated at Muncy, and by other Pennsylvania inmates, in a publication called *Graterfriends*, the newsletter of the Pennsylvania Prison Society. I thought the poems by these women prisoners in particular were quite good. (Three of them are reproduced at the end of chapter 12 of this volume.) I wrote asking if they might be interested in corresponding about the art of writing poetry. One of those I wrote to referred Sheena to me, and then Sheena, along with two of the others—Terri Harper and Kimberly Ayala—maintained a correspondence past a single exchange of letters. So I decided to go and pay them a visit.

Taking that step, the first step in getting to know these three women up close, beginning to develop friendships with each of them, has changed my life. I am hoping my own poem, shared below, written immediately after that first visit, will give you some idea of just how much.

In the course of our initial correspondence, Sheena mentioned a memoir that she had published online. I read it and was deeply moved. I suggested to her that we might usefully expand and develop what she had already written, then seek a wider circulation—because her story deserved a wider circulation. I remain convinced that the world will be a far better place after more people have become familiar with Sheena's story. That's true in particular because it's not just Sheena's story. It's the story of so many women who find themselves locked away in the prisons of the US because a chain of events in their lives began with childhood sexual abuse. This reality is a deep indictment of the so-called justice system our nation has constructed. Telling one of many such stories is not, of course, the only indictment we might make against what has aptly been called the "prison-industrial complex." But it is among the clearest, the most compelling on a human level. Now that you have read this book, I believe you will agree with that assessment.

I would also, by way of introduction after the fact, like to share something else that I have discovered as a result of my periodic visits to SCI Muncy, something that seems important to me. It is obvious that all of these inmates have much in common. But it is also true that each one remains an individual, who responds in her own unique way to the conditions of her incarceration. Prison life, I begin to understand, is a whole world unto itself, completely different from the world in which those of us who remain on the outside live. I now realize how difficult it is for most of us to comprehend the prison world—as difficult as it is to understand any culture of another nation, where people have different collective expectations, live a different kind of life. And just as in another nation, filled with people who share so much in common on a cultural level but who are also each individuals, so it is in a prison. Each prisoner, therefore, needs to be understood by the rest of us as an individual human being, not just as someone who is incarcerated. I had not, until now, taken the time necessary to realize this and act on it. If the same might be true of you, I offer these few words in hopes they will stimulate a bit of individual and collective self-reflection.

❦

Sheena acknowledges that she committed the act for which she is serving a life sentence. She is not asking for your sympathy or forgiveness, especially since she has still not forgiven herself for what she did. What she is asking for is your understanding—about why she did what she did, how we might change the world in ways that can keep others from making the same mistakes before it is too late.

It has been a privilege to work with Sheena King on this memoir, also to deepen my relationship with all the residents of SCI Muncy whom I have either met in person or heard stories about in the course of my visits. It has been a fascinating journey for me, one on which I know I have only begun. I expect my horizons to expand even more as I continue to travel in this strange country, attempting to understand its ways.

"Never stop learning and growing" has always been one of my personal mantras. Following it keeps me young. The same thought is, clearly, something that Sheena tries to convey to you in this book. If reading her memoir helps you to learn something new about the world, about yourself, and about the injustice of our present relationship with those who have broken society's laws (or have simply been accused and convicted, whether they have actually broken any laws or not), then I know Sheena will agree with me when I say it has been worth the struggle she had to go through to write this account of her life—and I mean all of the struggle, not just the struggle of the writing itself. So my personal thanks to those of you who have picked this from among so many books that you might choose to read, for deciding to accompany us on the journey.

❦

One final note: Sheena and I worked very hard to make sure the poems by her that appear on these pages were as polished and professional as possible. The poems by other inmates, however, are reproduced just as they came from the pens of their authors, individuals who have no formal training as writers—with only very minor editing for punctuation and similar technical matters. I personally believe that this adds to their importance as part of the documentation Sheena is attempting to provide, and to their impact. It's striking to me how good the writing is under the circumstances. If it still has flaws, then what we see is what we get. The whole package, positive and negative, is the product of our overwhelmingly abusive culture—which includes the culture of prison itself in addition to the culture of domestic abuse and childhood sexual abuse, all recounted in these verses.

Steve Bloom

There Is a Difference . . .

. . . between being opposed to war
and being a soldier in a war. This,
allow me to suggest, is not hard even
for those of us who have never been soldiers
to imagine.

There is also a difference
between being opposed to prisons
and being an inmate in a prison,
something most of us who have never
been inmates can, it seems likely,
imagine too
without much difficulty.

What I had never imagined
until today, however, is the difference
between being opposed to prisons and
simply paying a visit to one.

Walk through the razor wire for yourself,
however, as I did, this morning (for the first time),
feel what it is like to observe just a fraction
of the regulations, for only a few hours,
that residents of this edifice are expected
to abide by strictly, twenty-four hours each
and every day, some
for the rest of their lives.

And I believe that you, too, will find yourself
searching for words that might, somehow,
help us to comprehend.

About the Contributors

Sheena King is currently serving a life sentence at SCI Muncy in Muncy, Pennsylvania, where she is an advocate for incarcerated women, with degrees in religious studies and Christian counseling. She is the published author of a book of poems and journal entries titled *UnHeard Soul* and the novel *3Sum*. Her poems and essays have been published in journals and newspapers including *Let's Get Free, Daughters, The Philadelphia Inquirer, Pittsburgh Peace and Justice Newspaper, Prison Health News, Centers for Wisdom,* and *Tenacious*. Her work has also appeared in several anthologies, including *International Library of Poetry* and *Interrupted Life: Experiences of Incarcerated Women in the United States.*

Rikeyah Lindsay is healing justice organizer for Straight Ahead, the 501(c)(4) arm of the Abolitionist Law Center.

Victoria Law is a freelance journalist and author focused on incarceration, gender, and resistance. Her books include *Resistance Behind Bars: The Struggles of Incarcerated Women*; *Prison by Any Other Name: The Harmful Consequences of Popular Reforms*; and *Corridors of Contagion: How the Pandemic Exposed the Cruelties of Incarceration.*

Steve Bloom is a New York City–based poet, composer, and social activist. He is also the curator of the Poetry of Protest and Struggle video series that comes out three times each year; find it on YouTube. His website is stevebloompoetry.net.

ABOUT PM PRESS

PM Press is an independent, radical publisher of critically necessary books for our tumultuous times. Our aim is to deliver bold political ideas and vital stories to all walks of life and arm the dreamers to demand the impossible. Founded in 2007 by a small group of people with decades of publishing, media, and organizing experience, we have sold millions of copies of our books, most often one at a time, face to face. We're old enough to know what we're doing and young enough to know what's at stake. Join us to create a better world.

PM Press
PO Box 23912
Oakland, CA 94623
www.pmpress.org

PM Press in Europe
europe@pmpress.org
www.pmpress.org.uk

FRIENDS OF PM PRESS

These are indisputably momentous times—the financial system is melting down globally and the Empire is stumbling. Now more than ever there is a vital need for radical ideas.

In the many years since its founding—and on a mere shoestring—PM Press has risen to the formidable challenge of publishing and distributing knowledge and entertainment for the struggles ahead. With hundreds of releases to date, we have published an impressive and stimulating array of literature, art, music, politics, and culture. Using every available medium, we've succeeded in connecting those hungry for ideas and information to those putting them into practice.

Friends of PM allows you to directly help impact, amplify, and revitalize the discourse and actions of radical writers, filmmakers, and artists. It provides us with a stable foundation from which we can build upon our early successes and provides a much-needed subsidy for the materials that can't necessarily pay their own way. You can help make that happen—and receive every new title automatically delivered to your door once a month—by joining as a Friend of PM Press. And, we'll throw in a free T-shirt when you sign up.

Here are your options:

- **$30 a month** Get all books and pamphlets plus a 50% discount on all webstore purchases

- **$40 a month** Get all PM Press releases (including CDs and DVDs) plus a 50% discount on all webstore purchases

- **$100 a month** Superstar—Everything plus PM merchandise, free downloads, and a 50% discount on all webstore purchases

For those who can't afford $30 or more a month, we have **Sustainer Rates** at $15, $10 and $5. Sustainers get a free PM Press T-shirt and a 50% discount on all purchases from our website.

Your Visa or Mastercard will be billed once a month, until you tell us to stop. Or until our efforts succeed in bringing the revolution around. Or the financial meltdown of Capital makes plastic redundant. Whichever comes first.

Resistance Behind Bars: The Struggles of Incarcerated Women, 2nd Edition

Victoria Law with an Introduction by Laura Whitehorn

ISBN: 978-1-60486-583-7
$20.00 320 pages

In 1974, women imprisoned at New York's maximum-security prison at Bedford Hills staged what is known as the August Rebellion. Protesting the brutal beating of a fellow prisoner, the women fought off guards, holding seven of them hostage, and took over sections of the prison.

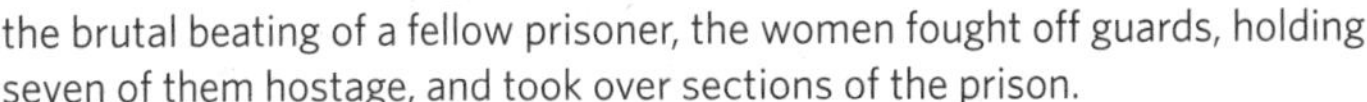

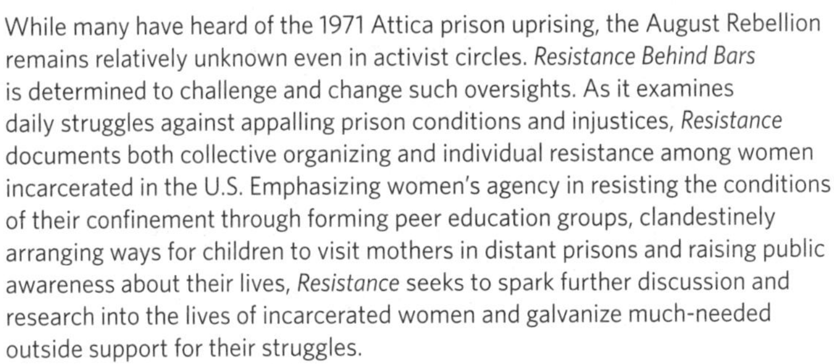

While many have heard of the 1971 Attica prison uprising, the August Rebellion remains relatively unknown even in activist circles. *Resistance Behind Bars* is determined to challenge and change such oversights. As it examines daily struggles against appalling prison conditions and injustices, *Resistance* documents both collective organizing and individual resistance among women incarcerated in the U.S. Emphasizing women's agency in resisting the conditions of their confinement through forming peer education groups, clandestinely arranging ways for children to visit mothers in distant prisons and raising public awareness about their lives, *Resistance* seeks to spark further discussion and research into the lives of incarcerated women and galvanize much-needed outside support for their struggles.

This updated and revised edition of the 2009 PASS Award-winning book includes a new chapter about transgender, transsexual, intersex, and gender-variant people in prison.

"Victoria Law's eight years of research and writing, inspired by her unflinching commitment to listen to and support women prisoners, has resulted in an illuminating effort to document the dynamic resistance of incarcerated women in the United States."
—Roxanne Dunbar-Ortiz

"Written in regular English, rather than academese, this is an impressive work of research and reportage"
—Mumia Abu-Jamal, death row political prisoner and author of *Live from Death Row*

"Finally! A passionately and extensively researched book that recognizes the myriad ways in which women resist in prison, and the many particular obstacles that, at many points, hinder them from rebelling. Even after my own years inside, I learned from this book."
—Laura Whitehorn, former political prisoner

A People's Guide to Abolition and Disability Justice

Katie Tastrom

ISBN: 979-8-88744-040-8 (paperback)
979-8-88744-054-5 (hardcover)
$19.95 / $29.95 256 pages

Disability justice and prison abolition are two increasingly popular theories that overlap but whose intersection has rarely been explored in depth.

A People's Guide to Abolition and Disability Justice explains the history and theories behind abolition and disability justice in a way that is easy to understand for those new to these concepts yet also gives insights that will be useful to seasoned activists. The book uses extensive research and professional and lived experience to illuminate the way the State uses disability and its power to disable to incarcerate multiply marginalized disabled people, especially those who are queer, trans, Black, or Indigenous.

Because disabled people are much more likely than nondisabled people to be locked up in prisons, jails, and other sites of incarceration, abolitionists and others critical of carceral systems must incorporate a disability justice perspective into our work. *A People's Guide to Abolition and Disability Justice* gives personal and policy examples of how and why disabled people are disproportionately caught up in the carceral net, and how we can use this information to work toward prison and police abolition more effectively. This book includes practical tools and strategies that will be useful for anyone who cares about disability justice or abolition and explains why we can't have one without the other.

"An essential movement tool. Tastrom convincingly shows that police and prison abolition and disability justice are core strategies for liberation and that we can't win one without the other."
—Alex Vitale, professor of sociology and coordinator of the Policing and Social Justice Project at Brooklyn College and the CUNY Graduate Center, and author of *City of Disorder* and *The End of Policing*

"A People's Guide to Abolition and Disability Justice *is a clear, accessible, and invaluable tool for not only dissecting the depths of disability and criminalization but also illustrating how the fights for disability justice and prison abolition are inextricably linked."*
—Victoria Law, author of *Resistance Behind Bars: The Struggles of Incarcerated Women* and *"Prisons Make Us Safer" & 20 Other Myths About Mass Incarceration*